A Friendly Tongue

From chips and shards in idle times
I made these stories, shaped these rhymes
May they engage some friendly tongue
When I am past the reach of song.

[Author's Note: The title for this book, *A Friendly Tongue*, comes from the verse above, from a poem by Byron Herbert Reece, a fine poet who taught at Young Harris College and died too young at age forty in 1958. He was a talented and tragic figure, aware at a young age that he had tuberculosis and would likely not live a full life span. That knowledge weighed on him, making him believe he could not with honor fall in love, marry, and raise a family.]

A Friendly Tongue

Hal Gulliver

with a Foreword
by *Tom Wicker*

ISBN 0-86554-118-3

*F
291.2
G85
1984*

A Friendly Tongue
Copyright © 1984
by Mercer University Press
Macon, Georgia 31207
All rights reserved
Printed in the United States of America

All books published by Mercer University Press
are produced on acid-free paper
that exceeds the minimum standards set by the
National Historical Publications and Records Commission.

Library of Congress Cataloging in Publication Data
Gulliver, Hal, 1935-
A friendly tongue.

"Essays . . . written for the Atlanta Constitution"—P.
Includes index.
1. Georgia—Politics and government—1951-
—Addresses, essays, lectures.
2. Southern States—Politics and government—1951-
—Addresses, essays, lectures.
3. Carter, Jimmy, 1924-
—Addresses, essays, lectures.
4. Southern States—Race relations—Addresses, essays, lectures.
I. Title.
F291.2.G85   1984   975.8'043   84-6733
ISBN 0-86554-118-3

Contents

Dedication

For Harold III

Foreword

Everybody knows that yesterday's newspaper is what they wrap the fish in. It follows that a collection of yesterday's newspaper articles is about as useful as a case of anthrax. Arthur M. Schlesinger, Jr. has denounced such stuff as worth little even for historical research, and I know a savant up in Vermont who buys the *New York Times* every day only because he's convinced that as garbage-can liner it repels raccoons more effectively than the *Rutland Herald*.

Why then, you will already have asked, this book by Hal Gulliver, who is known to have practiced journalism with both sexes, and why this introductory apology by another addict of that most despised deviation of our time? Even Gulliver himself incautiously included here a review of a collection of newspaper columns by a friend of his—no doubt I should say a former friend—in which he observed that the collection proved Shakespeare was right: "The evil men do lives after them, while the good is oft interred with their bones."

In quest of reasons for Gulliver's book, not to mention my role as accessory, I searched his ramblings to the end and was struck primarily by the fact that in a stingy list of journalists he admired, my name was not to be found. But audacity and dubious taste were ever the hallmarks of robust newspaper editing, particularly in what H. L. Mencken had the audacity and dubious taste to call the Sahara of the Bozart.

I was once told, for example, a story that ought to be true if it isn't, about an East Tennessee editor who referred in print to a local as a "son of a bitch." The alleged S.O.B. brought suit but, in a jury trial, lost the case. Thereafter the unappeased editor always referred to the unfortunate litigant as a "certified son of a bitch."

That's the kind of thing we regrettably don't get much of anymore even in the Sahara of the Bozart, which is now respectable and known as the Sunbelt. But there are a few other things to be said for Gulliver's exhumed articles from the *Atlanta Constitution* (a compendium from which he has shrewdly omitted the clinkers, the howlers, the "actionable," the predictions that failed, and the pieces about events of little current interest, like the 1971 Miss Teenage America Contest or the 1972 Arizona caucuses).

Gulliver had, in his prime, a certain rude Southern humor; see, for example, the story of the unorthodox appointment of one J. Phinias Archbolt to the Georgia bench by Governor Lester Maddox (September 8, 1969). Our author also defined a "great constitutional lawyer" as one who has made a lot of money losing segregation cases all the way up to the Supreme Court, and poked fun genially at politicians, lawyers, journalists, and other solemn asses.

Waxing serious when unable to avoid it, Gulliver—though confessing to Yankee antecedents—knew a thing or two about the South. Try this, from May 17, 1979.

> The very "best people" in the white community did some of the worst things. Don't ever believe the redneck types with cruel eyes were the ones who fought for segregation. They were lawyers who belonged to the best private clubs and accepted huge fees. . . . They were the school and college officials who took the witness stand in federal courts and lied under oath, insisting that their institutional policies were not really designed to maintain segregation. They were the ministers who preached in their churches on Sunday—oh, sometimes very subtly—that racism was the will of God.

Gulliver was not, like so many bloated pundits, entirely ignorant of politics. He published, on July 30, 1970, something close to a prediction that one Jimmy Carter was about to be elected governor of Georgia in November, taking care to point out that conventional wisdom had Carl Sanders far ahead; and by October 1975, not without a pardonable touch of state chauvinism, he had his neck pretty far out on the line that the same Carter would be the next president.

Other historical tidbits came his way and were duly committed to posterity: for example, the story of how Carter came to lose for governor instead of win for Congress in 1966, thereby starting on the road to the White House. And he has a serviceable stock of yarns with which to make a point, like the unfortunately true one about a black prison inmate who drowned in freezing waters because guards who were duck shooting had him swim out to retrieve their game. Georgia prison officials informed Governor Maddox that the black had jumped into the icy water because he enjoyed bringing back the ducks.

"You tell me how many people in Georgia believe that story," Maddox replied, "and I'll tell you how many fools there are in Georgia." (Gulliver, it should be noted, was not above finding the good as well as the axe handle in the likes of Maddox, whom he judged a dedicated prison reformer.)

In that most demanding of literary forms, the obituary, Gulliver displayed a Southerner's touch, combining a melancholy sense of the moment and proper respect for the deceased with irreverent recall of the lighter aspects of the subject's years. A good Southern funeral combines the laughter of life with the tears of death, and Gulliver managed to reproduce that atmosphere in his frequent eulogies.

In mitigation of his book, Gulliver pled in a note to readers that his stretch on the *Constitution*—roughly the twenty years after he cadged the job in 1962—were particularly interesting times. So they were, but I reject the argument; all times are particularly interesting, though some are more eventful than others. The evidence here is that Gulliver would have managed to make something out of a quieter era, too; he had the eye, the ear, the pen, and the gall.

Why go on? If the reasons cited can persuade busy people

to read these evidences that Gulliver once passed this way, that's their problem; if none of the above can make God-fearing persons move on to his resurrected lyrics and presentments, one can only conclude with the circulation department that the judgments of the subscribers are true and righteous altogether.

A final point. I have referred to Hal Gulliver in the past tense, not because he is legally dead, but because he is no longer writing for the *Atlanta Constitution*, hence no longer on expense account. For old newspapermen, the latter is a fate worse than death.

Tom Wicker
April 1984

Introduction

These essays were written for the *Atlanta Constitution* in the period from the late 1960s to the early 1980s, though in some ways they represent a full twenty-year stint with my favorite newspaper. I was a young reporter in 1962 when I joined the *Constitution*, an editor when I left in 1982. I was covering politics and civil rights and general foolishness in the early 1960s and columns written later drew on those experiences.

These pieces were all written under deadline pressure. That is by no means the worst way to write. It assures, at the least, fresh impressions and vivid detail; and it yields a picture of how something appeared exactly *then*, no matter how it might be analyzed later.

It was a fascinating time in the South, not a bad time to be around as a journalist. The essays in this book try to make plain some of the South's flavor, its good guys and bad guys, those things as deeply serious as Jerry Banks's broken heart and those best viewed with some humor. There is one thing of which I am certain: no matter how many New Souths continue to arise, Southerners have tended to make it through difficult times by keeping a sense of humor about themselves, especially their politics. Sometimes, either you laugh or you cry.

"Friend, given a proper budget and a free hand, I could sell dead cats to the State Board of Health," the illustrious Judge J. Wilton Carlyle once told me, summing up his political philosophy. Judge Carlyle appears sometimes in these pages. He did not quite exist in real life (whatever that is), but he closely resembles an old friend of mine, who shall be nameless here in order to protect the guilty.

I have grouped the essays in this volume in four sections. "Perspectives on (and from) the Deep South," the first section, includes pieces mainly on Southern politics and the civil rights revolution, though there are also a couple from as far away as Israel and South Africa. The second section, "Jimmy Carter's Time," includes columns on Carter's political career, from his underdog bid for governor to becoming—and serving—as the nation's thirty-ninth president. There is a fair amount of Judge Carlyle in this one. The third section, "Some Who Made a Difference," focuses on some remarkable individuals, some as well known as Robert Woodruff and Benjamin Mays, and Anwar Sadat, some not quite so well known perhaps, as Clarence Jordan and Clarence Bacote, Pinkie Masters and Bernice McCullar. The last section, "Personal Biases and Other Good Fun," is just what the title suggests.

The publication of this volume was made possible in part by a grant from the Watson-Brown Foundation, Inc.

Part I

Perspectives on (and from) the Deep South

Southern politics typically has had an element of mischief in it, color and outrageous rhetoric, often humor and good fun. A meanness of spirit surfaced on occasion too, usually involving racial issues. Demagogues of all descriptions played to racial prejudices for their own selfish ends. One exciting thing about Southern politics in the 1960s, 1970s, and early 1980s was the changing climate on this racial front. Racial biases still existed frequently enough, but it was no longer possible to parlay appeals to prejudice into elected office. On the contrary, new coalitions of white and black voters tended increasingly to reject such appeals and to vote for candidates promising to represent all citizens with fairness.

It was a surprising time. At the beginning of the period, Alabama Governor George Wallace was consolidating his white political base by literally standing in the schoolhouse door to oppose school integration; and yet, remarkably, this same George Wallace was by the end of the era winning election again as governor with a strong appeal for black voter support.

Similarly, it was hard to believe that a Lester Maddox could become governor of Georgia and a national figure almost solely by waving an ax handle around to keep blacks out of his restaurant. It was equally hard to believe his record as governor, which was a surprise in a different way. Maddox was aggressive in expanding welfare programs and seeking prison reform, two areas affecting proportionately more blacks than whites, and he compiled as good a record in naming new judges as any Southern governor of the time.

President Harry Truman wrote after leaving the White House that Senator Richard B. Russell of Georgia might very well have become president of the United States—if, that is, Russell had come from somewhere other than the South.

Nothing had changed much in this respect at the beginning of the era. But changes were going to come swiftly. In 1962 Dr. Martin Luther King, Jr. and Andrew Young lived in Atlanta; both were regarded as dangerous troublemakers by many white Americans. A fellow named Jimmy Carter of Plains decided that year to run for the State Senate. The only real public office he had previously held was on the local school board, a school board presiding over a racially segregated public school system. By the end of the era King had won the Nobel Peace Prize, died a martyr's death, and his birthday had become a national holiday. Carter had become governor of Georgia and then the thirty-ninth president of the United States, remarking often that only the civil rights revolution made it possible for a Southerner to become president. Young served as United Nations ambassador and chief spokesman for the administration policy of "human rights," relating that policy often to the Southern experience of the two decades just past.

It was, in all, a fine time to be with a newspaper like the *Atlanta Constitution* and to work with some splendid journalists who tried hard to make sense out of what was happening and to report it honestly.

How Georgia's
Political Climate
Is Changing

March 6, 1969

The winds of political change in Georgia often blow in a curious fashion. An attorney representing Georgia in a federal court case once said, speaking of Georgia politics, "It's been our experience that if it possibly can happen, well, it will."

This particular attorney, as it happens, is not to be confused with the illustrious line of Great Constitutional Lawyers who for years represented Georgia in fighting against various federal court decisions.

These distinguished authorities always lost their cases and always collected their high legal fees. After a time somebody decided that a regular state attorney from the attorney general's office could appear in federal court to lose a case just as easily as a Great Constitutional Authority. And it was a lot less expensive for the state.

That kind of change in the way we do things in Georgia is a minor one, really. But it's one of many. We have problems enough today in any number of areas, yet it's almost hard to comprehend that the compelling political issue in Georgia as recently as 1960—the year John F. Kennedy was elected president—was whether or not to close down the public schools. If you didn't close the schools down, after all, you might actually have some Negro youngsters sitting in classrooms with white children.

It's not likely that any Georgia political leader would attempt today to revive that line of argument, though school integration clearly is a source of continuing friction in most parts of the state.

Lester Maddox was elected governor with a reputation as an outspoken racist (though Maddox himself never raised racial questions during his 1966 campaign—the voters knew where he stood). Yet Gov. Maddox approved the naming of Negroes to local draft boards for the first time.

Former Gov. Carl Sanders won a national reputation as a moderate on racial matters while in office and, most observers thought, gave the state an improved national "image." But Sanders didn't really do anything much in the sense, say, of appointing Negroes to state boards or state jobs.

Governor Maddox reportedly once told a group of Negro leaders in his office: "If I do anything for you, it'll be more than the last fellow who sat in this chair did, and you helped him and didn't help me."

Maddox was right, of course, in one sense. But the Sanders contribution was of a different kind. Sanders changed the political rhetoric of the state. He steadfastly refused, for the most part, to use the conventional racist phrases so dearly loved by many Georgia politicians. He helped change the political climate.

One sign of this changed climate is apparent in the current move to restore Georgia's 1879 state flag. Our present flag features the stars and bars of the Confederacy with the state seal at one end. It was adopted by the legislature in the 1950s, when former Gov. Marvin Griffin was in office, and in a kind of general way, the change was supposed to indicate Southern patriotism and an undying belief in segregation.

State Rep. Janet Merritt of Americus says the Confederate flag is an "honored part of our past," but that it has no place as part of the Georgia state flag. She has introduced a bill restoring the 1879 flag, which was designed by veterans of the Civil War.

The fascinating thing is that, whatever the outcome, this kind of bill is not really an emotional issue in this year's General Assembly.

Legislators are sweating it out on a compromise tax plan, an appropriations bill, educational programs, penal reform, a host of matters. But one measure of our changed political climate is that a debate over even the Confederate flag doesn't seem likely to erupt in a series of fiery, table-thumping, arm-waving political speeches. We should be grateful.

It Happened
in Chicago

March 20, 1969[1]

The good Maj. Sartoris and Capt. Compton are friends again, I think, though it was probably a near thing for a while there in Chicago. But they came up through the state patrol together, and the major already knew that Compton had a good-humored streak of devilment in him. Let me tell it this way. The Secret Service man stood in one corner of the wide hotel suite, looking a little like a small-town undertaker or an FBI agent. A sympathetic undertaker, nonetheless, and Capt. Compton decided this was the time to confide in him.

The captain led into it gently, keeping a straight face as best he could. A Democratic National Convention was enough to make a man nervous, he said, especially if you happened to come from the Deep South. Also, it got a lot more complicated

---

[1] It was a shortlived, unlikely campaign, but indeed then-Governor Lester Maddox of Georgia did announce for president in 1968, and went to the National Democratic Convention as a candidate with Secret Service protection. This account is accurate; the names have been changed to protect the guilty.

guarding a man who was governor-and-presidential-candi-
date all at the same time.

The captain noted that he himself was only, you might say,
temporarily in charge of security, as far as the state patrolmen
with the governor were concerned. But Maj. Sartoris, an out-
standing man, the very pride of the state patrol, in fact, was
flying into Chicago that day to take personal charge.

The Secret Service man nodded agreeably and said he
would certainly look forward to working with the major.

There was just one small problem, the captain continued,
looking uneasy, and he thought it well to mention it before
Maj. Sartoris arrived. The major was probably one of the best
law-enforcement men of all time but, well, as it happened, the
major was also an incurable alcoholic, said the captain.

(Now, gentle reader, pay attention. Note the evil-but-good-
natured glint in the captain's eye. Don't take him as seriously
as did the Secret Service man.)

The governor, of course, doesn't drink at all, Capt. Compton went on, so you can see how embarrassing it would be for
him if Maj. Sartoris got hold of a drink of whiskey and disap-
peared for three or four days.

It occurred to the Secret Service man that the governor
would not be the only person embarrassed. And, he thought
longingly, they could have assigned me to Nixon or Humphrey,
or even George Wallace.

They were distracted momentarily, as the governor
emerged from the bedroom where he'd gone to change his
shirt, and started out the door to confound another delegation
or two.

Sure enough, Maj. Sartoris arrived that day and moved
quickly to take charge. The Secret Service man was impressed
with his clear-eyed vigor. You just never know, he thought to
himself.

Both state law officers and Secret Service men were working twelve-hour days or better, and were clearly under some
pressure. They, naturally, were all cold sober and dedicated
while on duty, but there were those among them who at the end

of a long day were inclined to take a small glass of cheer, usually in the form of bourbon and water.

There were hospitality rooms aplenty in the convention hotels, and at the end of that first long day, the good Maj. Sartoris
(now off duty) appeared in one such oasis and was offered a
brimming glass.

The first warming sip never reached his lips. Just then, a
Secret Service man (carefully briefed) walked over and took the
glass firmly from his hand. Maj. Sartoris was a little baffled
at this, especially after the same thing happened several other
times in the next two days, but he took it with reasonably good
grace, thinking it was just another high-level security
precaution.

It was on the third day that the light slowly dawned. It took
some doing to convince the Secret Service that actually he was
not, and never had been, an alcoholic.

Then, he sought out his old friend Capt. Compton (whose
amusement was great) for some personal conversation. Unfortunately, the conversation cannot be reproduced in a family
newspaper.

Moral: Isn't this just the kind of story some lyin' Atlanta
newspaperman might make up?

Georgia Schools
and Mr. Nixon's
Southern Strategy

May 19, 1969[2]

As a Georgia legislator said once, referring to the State Highway Department, "You just can't take politics out of politics."

The same truth applies to school desegregation. It's not a question of whether such an issue should be in politics. It's simply a fact that it is. President Nixon, an astute political animal, finally reached the White House in part because he pursued a so-called "Southern strategy." It succeeded. Southern conservatives like South Carolina Sen. Strom Thurmond campaigned for Nixon all over the South, insisting again and again that Nixon had a segregationist heart, close to that of Alabama's George Wallace.

---

[2]This column was too optimistic in suggesting that the appointment of Leon Panetta signaled the direction of the Nixon administration on school desegregation. It was true enough that Panetta did not support delaying tactics on desegregation, and for that very reason the White House fired him in early 1970. He was later elected to the United States Congress from California.

Candidate Nixon contributed to this impression by suggesting that "local" school boards should run local schools. The political message was clear, in context, and the message was: "You good folk listen to what Strom says. Don't go wasting your vote on George Wallace."

Well, Mr. Nixon isn't the first man to hint at one thing in a campaign and then crawfish on it once in office. It's an honored political tradition. In terms of the presidency, it's probably a good thing: that high office has a tendency to bring out the best in any politician. Most men holding that office have tended to shrug off campaign promises and have, apparently, tried hard to make decisions in the national interest. But, still, you can understand why a good many Southern Republicans felt they had something like a promise that the process of school integration would be slowed down—even reversed—with President Nixon in the White House. After all, didn't Nixon carry Florida, Tennessee, Virginia, South Carolina, and North Carolina? Hubert Humphrey could claim, by comparison, only Texas in the original states of the Confederacy. Wallace got the rest.

President Nixon—as distinguished from Candidate Nixon—seemed for a time to avoid decisions on school integration. That is, he left the impression that he wanted to maintain his warm ties with Southern segregationists like Strom Thurmond—yet not really change the school integration guidelines administered by the Department of Health, Education, and Welfare. The administration couldn't have it both ways, of course. Maybe the decisive clue came when Leon Panetta, a young California attorney, was named a few weeks ago to head HEW'S Office for Civil Rights. Panetta, who's been active in California politics, is considered a liberal . . . and unlikely to support any delaying tactics on school desegregation.

He came to Georgia last Friday, primarily to meet with a group of Georgia school superintendents. It's his first such confrontation on that scale since he assumed his new responsibilities. Panetta is a soft-spoken man, has dark hair, wears glasses, and seems both diplomatic and courteous. But what he said ought to make clear—even to the most obtuse—that the

Nixon Administration has no intention of changing the process of school integration. As he commented, it would be a "tragic charade" for the administration to "wink at this law and still call for law and order on college campuses and in the streets." He said the federal mandate calling for complete integration of schools by this September will be "strictly enforced." Panetta added, "A lot of people, especially in the South, felt that Strom [Thurmond] was going to run HEW."

Well, that's certainly what Strom thought.

Playing the Game
by the Old Rules

September 8, 1969

Colonel J. Phinias Archbolt, well-known counselor-at-law in several militia districts, was in his office one day recently when his secretary came in and told him the governor's office was on the telephone.

"Why am I calling the governor's office?" he demanded suspiciously, glaring at his secretary. His secretary, a demure, bright-eyed young lady, responded a little breathlessly. "You're not calling him," she said. "It's his office. The governor is calling you."

Now, J. Phinias Archbolt had been an active—if inept— dabbler in politics for many, many years. He'd talked to more than one governor in his time, but he'd never talked to this governor and, truth to tell, never even planned to talk to him. It was J. Phinias's view that the present governor was a Great Political Accident, a dangerous, wildman nonpolitician who in some incredible fashion had parlayed a few loose ax handles into the governor's chair. It wasn't the man's opinions that made J. Phinias think he was dangerous, but the question of not playing by the rules. The governor didn't even know anybody in Georgia politics, J. Phinias thought. It was outrageous, he decided, peering at the old Eugene Talmadge photograph on the wall. The idea that anybody got to be governor without knowing more than two or three state legislators by name . . . well, it just ran counter to all the things J. Phinias loved and held dear.

"I don't want to talk to the governor," snorted J. Phinias, gazing upward at the old Elect M. E. Thompson poster in one corner. "Ask his secretary what they want." J. Phinias's secretary, dutiful girl that she was, went back to the telephone, talked for a moment and rushed back, her eyes wide, saying, "That's not a secretary. It's the governor himself. He says he wants to make you a judge." "Make me a judge?" roared J. Phinias, his eyes focusing with difficulty on the framed document making him a member of Gov. Marvin Griffin's staff. "He can't do that. What's that fellow up to? Why does he want to make me a judge?"

Now, J. Phinias had wanted to be a judge for years and years. However, he knew the rules. First you campaigned for somebody who got elected governor, then maybe with luck you got to a judge. Some fine lawyers got appointed sometimes. He gazed grimly at the photograph of J. Phinias shaking hands with Gov. Vandiver . . . only trouble was he'd collected all his mementos after elections, after he'd gone down in flames with various losing candidates.

"Tell the governor I was on the Ellis Arnall Campaign Committee," said J. Phinias, sighing, peering down at his Carl Sanders Christmas cufflinks. "The governor says you're the best qualified attorney in the area," his secretary said, after talking on the phone again.

J. Phinias stood up from his chair, pounding on the desk with one fist. "Tell the governor I was a Democrat-for-Callaway in the general election," he said. "The governor says he knows all that. He says the Georgia Bar Association recommends you highly." "What's that got to do with it?" shouted J. Phinias. "That's fellow's trying to undermine the state's whole political system. Tell him I voted against George Wallace. Tell him I drink whiskey."

His secretary talked on the telephone again, then stared over at J. Phinias. "The governor says he wants to swear you in tomorrow afternoon," she said. J. Phinias sat back in his chair, a beaten man, staring at the wall (at one of the few portions of wall not covered by political mementos). So, he was going to be a judge. "Tell the governor just one other thing," said J. Phinias. "Tell him I said Phooey."

But he knew he'd be in Atlanta the next day, in time for his swearing-in ceremony.

On Becoming
Atlanta's Most
Visible Minority

October 30, 1969[3]

It wasn't absolutely clear to me at first what being a member of the perhaps now most noticeable minority group in Atlanta meant.

My young son telephoned me at the office one afternoon several days after the mayor's election was over and asked, "Why am I a bee?" Now, the question came in a small, serious voice, so I proceeded cautiously. "Why are you a bee?" I repeated, slowly, thinking suddenly that my son had heard someone talking about the birds and the bees and had gotten mixed up. "You are a bee, too," my son continued. "I am?" I said, still in confusion, though reflecting there may well be those who think of me as a Son of a Bee.

To my great relief the small lad's mother came on the line. "He doesn't mean bee," she said. "He means wasp."

---

[3]This was written after Sam Massell was elected mayor of Atlanta, the city's first Jewish mayor. Atlanta was on its way to becoming a majority black city, and Massell won with substantial black support.

"Wasp? You mean like flying-in-the-air wasp?" said I, in some disbelief.

"No, no," she said. "Not small letters, wasp. Big letters, WASP. Like flying-over-to-the-Piedmont-Driving-Club WASP."

There was a moment's small silence.

"Well," I said, seeing my duty to explain clearly, "You are a WASP, and that means White Anglo-Saxon Protestant, and your mother will tell you what that means. I've got to do some work." "Coward," came a mother's voice, as I hung up the phone.

I had another call a little later, this time from a business-man downtown, one who happened to be Jewish and sup-ported the losing candidate in the mayor's race. "It's terrible," he said. "When I go to the Standard Club, people point at me and say bad things." He paused for a moment, and I thought I heard a quiet sob. "You know, someone Jewish finally takes over something, and I'm on the other side. It's not fair," he roared.

After a moment he calmed down and asked if I could come to a party at his home the next weekend. "You know, just a few friends," he said. "There will be at least one other WASP couple there, so you won't feel uncomfortable."

"Kind of a token WASP delegation?" I suggested.

"No, no," he said. "You know, some of my best friends are. . . ."

"Don't say it," I said.

There was one more telephone call. A well-known black state senator telephoned me late in the afternoon.

"You know, we're still friends, whatever the results of any election. In fact," he went on, waxing enthusiastic, "some of my best friends live in Sandy Springs."

"But I don't live in Sandy Springs." I objected.

"Well, you know what I mean," he said. "Places like that."

"You mean places where the WASPs gather, so we can be with our own kind?"

"Now, don't be sarcastic," the senator said. "As you know, I think your group has contributed a lot to our city. I think, really, that there's certainly a place for members of your group in Atlanta's future."

"Well, that's white of you," I said, regretting it immediately. But the good senator laughed.

"Just don't worry about anything," he said. "I really just wanted you to know that you'll always have a friend in City Hall."

How South Africa Is Similar to the Old South

September 17, 1971

PRETORIA, SOUTH AFRICA—Prime Minister B. J. Vorster has offices in this administrative capital in one square corner of the solid old stone Union Buildings.

If Vorster walks to his office windows, he can look out over this sprawling city of just under half a million people. It's spring here, the beginning of spring, and the light rains are starting to turn the grass green. In a few weeks the purple jacaranda trees will blossom and, as one South African put it, "submerge the whole city beneath a cloud of blue."

From his offices Vorster can look to the low hills on the other side of Pretoria and see, just barely, the outline of the memorial structure erected in memory of the late prime minister, his predecessor, Dr. H. F. Verwoerd, who was shot down in 1966. It's not on record that Prime Minister Vorster is given to such musings, but he could well say to himself, while peering at the memorial to Verwoerd: *What exactly did you put into motion, doctor? And where will it end?*

Many South Africans are, in any case, asking such questions. There are intense discussions, public and private, about the future of South African racial policies.

"I told a friend once that Dr. Verwoerd was really a liberal," chortled one government official, in private conversation, conscious of how contrary-to-image that might sound. In fact, Dr. Verwoerd was the Apostle of Apartheid—the solid, stolid, confident prophet of the white master race in South Africa. And yet Dr. Verwoerd set in motion some political forces, quite consciously, whose outcome seems ambiguous at best.

Verwoerd, certainly, invented neither segregation nor apartheid. In this country the color bar was enshrined in the South Africa Act of 1909. But it was Verwoerd's political party, the Nationalist party, which came to power in 1948 and began taking an active interest in a mass of laws and regulations with racial implications that, taken together, were called apartheid. Verwoerd, a brilliant man by all reports, a professor and a sociologist, became prime minister of his party in 1958. He then, for the first time, began seemingly to take the idea of "separate development" of the black citizens of South Africa seriously.

It was as if a Southern governor in the United States, prior to the 1954 school decision, suddenly decided to take the idea of separate-but-equal schools seriously, moving in that vein to upgrade all-black schools. Indeed, Georgia Gov. (at the time) Herman Talmadge, whatever his political rhetoric, moved somewhat in this direction, acting to equalize black and white teacher salaries in the early 1950s.

The comparison between South Africa and the American South only reaches so far; I probably overstate it already, so take warning. But it is simply flat true that the political climate in South Africa has shifted in the last several years, in ways that don't seem to be often reported in American newspapers.

For example, only a relatively short time ago, the words *conservative* and *liberal* had come to have much the same meaning in this country as they did politically in the South. That is, "liberal" had a quite unpopular connotation to many people, smacking of a left-wing, semi-Communist, and of one suspiciously soft on racial matters. "Conservative" had the more solid sound, specifically including a strong segregationist line.

Today, some interesting new political words have taken hold. As Deon Fourie, a senior political lecturer at the University of South Africa, explained it to me, a political speaker not too long ago criticized some men in the ruling Nationalist party for having "cramped" thinking.

Now, here a language explanation is necessary. There are two official languages in the Republic of South Africa, Afrikaans and English, the former evolving from seventeenth-century Dutch and the mother tongue of about sixty percent of the white people. About half the major newspapers are published in English, half in Afrikaans. Virtually every white citizen speaks fluent English and Afrikaans.

Well, the word used for "cramped" thinking was "verkramp." Another word used was "verlig," meaning roughly "enlightened" and referring to the more progressive—on racial issues—segment of the party in power. The fascinating thing is not that *verkramp* would presumably be the more conservative term, *verlig* the more liberal. Surprisingly, to an outsider, most influential members of the government, including the prime minister, want to consider themselves *verlig*.

In fact, some conservative members of the party, the more *verkramp*, broke away in protest, even starting a newspaper and a new party, the Herstigte Nationale party.

The most spectacular example of what this more *verlig* policy might mean came in late August when South Africa hosted an official visit from a black African leader, President Kamuzu Banda of Malawi, with all appropriate protocol and honors and official banquets (though it's not clear he was even an Honorary White).

The Herstigte Nationale party newspaper ran a picture of South African soldiers paying honor-guard tribute to President Banda. The headline, written no doubt in great unhappiness, "Whites Salute Black."

How a State Senator Finally Did Right

July 4, 1972

BOSTON—This city is a reasonably far piece away from Atlanta to come to hear a story about a small Southern town, a town sounding like south Georgia, with the courthouse and courthouse square at the center of things.

The courthouse square was Southern all right, but it was in Louisiana. The man telling the story, Jesse Stone, was an attorney and some fifteen years ago had just begun his practice in Shreveport. He originally came from a much smaller town.

"I went back to my home town on a case. Not a civil rights case, though it had a racial issue," he said. "A black woman had been injured by a white man and was suing for damages."

Stone, a tall, wide black man, would be fairly visible in any crowd. There was a crowd in front of the courthouse when he arrived, a closely knit crowd literally filling all the space outside the courthouse.

"I had to push my way through. Very slowly, because I didn't want to get anybody excited. But I had to get to the courtroom, and I had to push between people to get past," he remembered.

No one actually tried to do Stone any harm. It was a group
of people, white, who gave off the decided impression that they
really weren't yet accustomed to the idea of a black attorney
from Shreveport, native son or not, there to try a case just like
a regular lawyer.

"I didn't know quite what to expect," Stone remembers.

The white judge sitting on the bench looked at him after he
came into the courtroom, got up from his chair and walked
around and then went up to Stone . . . to shake his hand and
speak to him in a courteous fashion. Somehow, by the time
Stone walked out again, the word had moved around the
crowd. People moved aside and created a wide path for him. "It
was just that gesture that did it, the judge coming down to
shake hands with me," he believes, and he has thought about it
since—how that one small courtesy had a psychological effect
way out of proportion to its surface meaning. Indeed, so often
in the South seemingly small things can affect the complicated, often tortuously difficult, relationship between black
people and white people, in an era when much of the racism
and racial discrimination of the past is being slowly changed
for the better.

Stone, as a practicing and successful black attorney, has
found himself involved in Louisiana politics at most election
times, both in local and state campaigns. Once, he probably
could have gone to the state legislature, a sometime ambition
of his. But when the opportunity came, he decided that really
wasn't what he wanted and supported a black friend, who was
elected to the seat.

He remembers a time when he and others decided to try to
muster black voters' support for a white state senator, one
with a segregationist record.

"He had been a segregationist, and a strong one, but he
had a reputation for being honest and doing what he had
promised. He said he'd do right if we'd support him. We were
supporting some younger, less experienced candidates for the
legislature, and we thought this senator might give the local
delegation more strength," he said.

The senator won reelection with black voter help. Asked if the senator then "did right," Stone grinned. "I remember when some segregationist legislation came up after that. This senator had a conservative reputation. He stood up and said, 'I went down that road once before. I'm not going that way any more.' It made people sit up and listen."

Stone, on a television panel in Boston to talk about the "New South," is part of what that New South is about. He's now assistant state school superintendent of Louisiana, an able and competent and well-respected man. "I can remember," he says, "when I first started practicing law, and I had a young son, and I thought that I wanted to do things, some of them, so that my son would never have to face some of the things I had faced." Stone's son died earlier this year, at nineteen, in an automobile accident. It is a safe bet, though, that he was proud of his dad.

Burying Democrats
Only When
They're Dead

July 31, 1972[4]

Zell Miller, the young ex-history professor who now serves as executive director of the Georgia Democratic party, has the curious idea that being a Democrat actually ought to involve supporting Democratic candidates for public office, up to and including the Democratic nominee for president of the United States. It is a revolutionary thought for Georgia Democrats, who function best at hiding out or copping out during a national election year.

Miller spoke out in a civic club speech last Friday. Sen. George McGovern is not as conservative as Miller would like, but he intends to support him, given that choice or four more years of a Republican administration in Washington. Miller contends that many of the McGovern boosters, including those in the Georgia delegation at the Miami national convention, have gotten a bum rap.

---

[4]Zell Miller's feisty political style appealed to many Georgia voters. He was elected lieutenant governor of Georgia in 1974 and reelected to that post in 1978 and 1982.

"Frankly," said Miller, who was there in Miami, "those in the Georgia delegation were not the types of person you have been led to believe make up the McGovern forces. In Georgia, they included a respected Presbyterian minister, a sixty-seven-year-old retired mail clerk (the oldest person in the delegation), a middle-aged housewife who never before had engaged in any kind of politics, and a brilliant college math major from Duluth who has worked her way through college and in 1968 voted for Richard Nixon.

"Communists? Traitors to our country? Welfare bums? Hippies?

"Not hardly."

Most of the McGovern backers, Miller went on, seemed to be "persons who are participating in the affairs of government—participating, most for the first time with no axes to grind, with no thought of political or financial advancement. That's bad? Had you rather have the wheeler-dealers, the fat cats, the smoke-filled room brand of politics?

". . . I am a history teacher who happens to have gotten involved in politics, not a politician who happens to have read a little history, and so I am not overly disturbed at these 'sunshine Democrats' who are now wringing their hands in despair and threatening to leave the Democratic party. This is nothing new in Georgia political history. The noises they are making now have the same sound as in 1948 when Harry Truman was too liberal, in the 1950s when Adlai Stevenson was too liberal, in 1960 when John Kennedy was too liberal, and so on in 1964 and 1968."

Most of the "so-called leaders" of the Georgia Democratic party who threaten not to support the national Democratic ticket, Miller went on, never have supported it in the past. "Their actions are like those of a dog who chases cars. He'll bark after the car until it's out of sight. Then he'll come back wagging his tail, with a smug look on his face as if his barking caused that car to go down the street."

Miller suggests that McGovern's position has been distorted on some issues. The Nixon administration's Justice Department had 214 school desegregation cases pending last

December, all but seven in the South. HEW, under the GOP, he said, has initiated 550 proceedings against school systems, all but nine in the South. Do Georgians want this, asked Miller, "or do they want a man [McGovern] who has stood on Georgia soil and advocated uniform—yes, uniform—application of civil rights acts and voting rights acts?"

The things Miller said will undoubtedly make some Georgia Democrats angry. Being a shrewd political man, Miller knows the odds in Georgia and nationally against McGovern. But he tells the story of some citizens years ago who believed President Andrew Jackson ought to have a suitable coffin and, at great expense, bought a huge marble box that weighed about five tons. Trouble was, Andrew Jackson wasn't dead yet and wasn't much interested. "I must decline the intended honor," he wrote to the citizens.

"And they never did get old Hickory in that thing," said Miller. "You can still see it if you're interested, out in front of the Smithsonian Institute in Washington where it still sits. The moral of this little tale is this: Before you bury a Democrat, you had better be sure he is dead."

Troubling
White Liberal
Draws Investigation

September 28, 1972

There is nothing, just nothing that makes a good, white
moderate-to-liberal sort more out of sorts than being pushed
into being more liberal than he wants to be.

Your white liberal, after all, knows that his heart is right.
He tries to do the decent thing. He often does. He believed in
human-relations councils and all those things back when they
were really controversial. He admires the late Dr. Martin Luther King, Jr., especially now that he's dead and safely a martyr and unlikely to turn up next Tuesday saying disturbing
things.

Now, the Rev. Austin Ford is the kind of idiot troublemaker
who drives your good Northside-Atlanta white liberal up the
wall. Ford is obviously a knee-jerk Episcopalian type put in
the world solely to promote foolishness and create consterna-
tion, particularly among good and decent upper-middle-class
people who are trying to do right.

Ford more or less heads something called Emmaus House,
which is somehow more or less financed and supported by the
Episcopal Diocese of Atlanta. Somehow, Ford seems mostly to

get mixed up with what are called "social issues," usually involving poor people or black people. He even acts as if he likes them. And there are apparently enough bubbleheaded Episcopalians in Atlanta to put up with Ford's messing around in all kinds of things and ending up half the time in some kind of controversy. However, some of the more solid and respectable Episcopalians recently helped promote a committee to investigate Ford.

The latest thing he's involved in is fairly outrageous. As we all know and don't often say, Atlanta's school system has finished with desegregation and has now reached that high level of de facto segregation achieved long ago by more sophisticated Northern cities like New York and Chicago; if you're a white semiliberal, that is the best of all worlds. You can be in favor of federal court orders and equally in favor of the residential patterns, which mean that your school is mostly white. The Rev. Ford has had the audacious, outrageous gall to buck the pattern by encouraging poor black students to transfer from predominantly black inner-city schools to predominantly white Northside Atlanta schools.

Rector Frank M. Ross of All Saints Church in Atlanta took due note in his church bulletin last Sunday, saying:

> Dearly Beloved Brethren: I want to write a word about the Rev. Austin Ford, Emmaus House and some Northside Atlanta public schools. As I understand it, any child in the Atlanta school system can transfer, using proper procedures, from a majority racial position to a minority racial position. This is part of the desegregation processes in this system.
>
> Father Ford has provided the encouragement to a number of people in the Stadium area to transfer their children to Northside elementary schools. This gives two differing groups of children the chance to learn together in numbers beyond the token. There is some indication that initially the academic processes are disturbed. I suppose you would expect this for both groups of children.
>
> However, I have a son at Morris Brandon School, one of the schools involved. A lot of hard work from some parents stabilized things last year. This year promises to be an exciting one. My son is being enriched by all of this and I am grateful

to Austin Ford. It's called Christian leadership. Faithfully,
Frank M. Ross, Rector.

Who is this Ross anyway? What does he know? Probably
just another one of those troublesome Episcopalian liberals.

Watergate Climate Creates Tragic Political Impact

August 20, 1973

One of the evil, literally evil, influences of the Watergate
scandal relates to the repeated suggestion that, well, bad as it
all seems, isn't that the way politics usually is? Isn't this typical? Aren't we really just saying that these friends and associates of President Nixon were caught in the act, so to speak,
but in actions that other politicians have committed without
being caught?

One of the witnesses before the Senate committee, a lower-
level ex-White House staff member, was asked how he would
advise young people considering government service. "Don't
do it," he said, smarting under the TV lights and the thoughts
of where his White House stint had brought him.

A U.S. senator said in private talk recently that one of his
constituents, a Methodist minister, had visited him in Washington not long ago, while the Watergate hearings were un-
derway, and had suggested this point of view, that the Nixon
boosters facing serious charges had done probably just exactly
what other politicians had done.

Well, the senator told the minister, that really wasn't true. The politicians he knew simply did not typically authorize burglary, or violate other laws, or perjure themselves under oath, or try in various ways to obstruct justice.

The Methodist minister was polite about it, the senator said later, but clearly remained unconvinced. Yet I suspect that almost anyone who has worked in any fashion around political people, people in government at whatever level, understands that this Watergate-engendered climate is wrong, wrong and inaccurate.

It just isn't true that people in public office are typically crooks and rogues. There are crooks and rogues enough to go around, to be sure, but that's true of the world in general as well as the world of government and politics.

Journalists tend to be suspicious of politicians. They're supposed to be. Yet most journalists who have covered politics can testify that the thoroughgoing crooks are the exception rather than the rule. For every politico who sells his vote for a favor to make the fast buck, there are dozens who work fairly hard at politics and government, who do the best they can, who aren't trying to steal money or in any other fashion trying to violate the law in order to enhance their own power or prestige.

This part of the Watergate fallout, the creation of a climate suggesting the crookedness of all politics and politicians, is simply tragic. It is tragic because the impact of it is to discourage good people, qualified people, from seeking public office (a consideration of particular significance in Atlanta this week as candidates qualify for mayor, city council president, city council seats, and school-board positions).

Helen Bullard, who has worked as a political consultant in many campaigns, is fond of observing that any political campaign is so extraordinarily demanding on the individual candidate that we—people generally—owe a real debt of gratitude to qualified candidates who seek office, whether they win or lose. That is especially true today in this sour Watergate climate, a climate created not by the press or by Richard Nixon's political enemies, but by that select, lawless, unscrupulous band of Nixon's personal friends and associates who never hesitated in invoking the awesome, direct powers of the presidency to the shoddiest possible political ends.

Thinking
of Cedar Trees,
Oysters, and Turtles

*April 24, 1977**

Cedar Key is a lovely spot along the Florida coast (a small island, really connected to the mainland now by a causeway) that is boating-and-fishing-oriented and has about as pleasant a sleepy-old-town look as there is to be found in Florida.

No new motels or hotels much, nothing very modern in appearance, except maybe boats, and some splendid new boats, some belonging to local folk, some to the people who drive from as far away as Atlanta to get there (a good seven hours, if you make good time).

Cedar Key is a glorious spot, and I find myself grateful to my neighbor, Charlie King, a basic boat freak, for introducing me to such a pleasant place. It comes to mind in thinking about President Jimmy Carter's energy speech last week, and the howls from some who just don't want to believe that American life-styles may have to change.

---

*This essay originally appeared in the Sunday *Atlanta Journal and Constitution*.

Cedar Key got its name because a century ago there were literally great groves of cedar trees on the land, beautiful trees of superb wood. Along about 1880 someone erected a pencil factory. The factory did a marvelous business, cutting down those big cedar trees and making them into pencils. The process took about five years. In five years, the great groves of cedar trees were mostly gone and did not grow again in anything like the speed necessary to provide a continuing supply. Oh, the pencil factory went on for a few years; there were other cedar trees nearby, but they too gave out after a while.

There are not any cedars on Cedar Key now, not to amount to anything. Mostly there are pines, other trees that grew in more rapidly.

A couple of other things happened to Cedar Key in that period of its heyday. There used to be numbers of large green turtles in those waters. Fishermen caught them in huge numbers and sent them to faraway spots, most prominent perhaps the famous Fulton Fish Market in New York City, where they were sold as gourmet treats. After a time, the green turtles were about fished (or caught) out. That industry vanished, like the cedar trees. The same thing happened with sponges, also an industry at the time in that area. The same thing happened—can you believe?—with the oyster beds, fished out in a very few years.

Well, the oyster beds have been reseeded in recent years, and the oysters and the sea food are delicious indeed (the stone crabs are incredible). But the cedars are still gone. And the sponges. And the green sea turtles.

It occurs to me that this nation has been living with our energy sources for the last couple of decades in about the same way the the exploiters of Cedar Key lived with their groves of trees not quite a century ago. And the way they lived with the sponges, and oysters, and sea turtles.

It is a time that will not last. The pencil factories will close down. No matter what action the Congress takes on President Carter's energy program, we are in a time of seeing existing resources vanish away, be used up. Many do not want to believe it. That's probably how some of the workers at the pencil factory on Cedar Key felt.

Biko's Murder: Ominous Prophecy of Tragic Events

September 19, 1977

In a moment this gets around to South Africa and the tragic death of a young man, a death with dire implications for the future of that nation, but it starts, perhaps in an unlikely fashion, with former Gov. Lester Maddox. He was not everyone's cup of tea as governor of Georgia, of course, and maybe his record was an uneven one in various ways, but ole Lester had some proud moments indeed.

One occurred after a black prison inmate in a country public-work camp had been callously used as a hunting dog by prison guards. That is, the guards were duck shooting in frigid weather and it seemed perfectly reasonable in their minds to have a black prisoner swim out in icy waters to retrieve their game. There is no record of how many times prisoners were abused in that fashion, but on one cold day a prison inmate drowned in the freezing waters.

The facts of the case did not surface immediately, and when they did prison authorities at first denied that there had been any abuse of the prisoner. He had jumped in that icy water to bring back the ducks because he enjoyed it, prison officials asserted.

Lester Maddox as governor was outraged, in quite a proper humane spirit, and would have none of such phoney explanations. "You tell me how many people in Georgia believe that story, and I'll tell you how many fools there are in Georgia," declared Maddox. Maddox in various ways as governor pressed for prison reform about as vigorously as any Georgia governor ever has.

Officials of the white South African government object bitterly when U. N. Ambassador Andrew Young or anyone else compares the racist policies of the South African government to the racist patterns of segregation existing in the South until only a few years ago. But the death of a young black South African last week, thirty-year-old Steven Biko, offers unhappy echoes of the way black civil rights leaders were sometimes treated in the American South a few years ago. Maddox, a declared segregationist, often demonstrated what someone once called "zones of decency" and spoke up more passionately against mistreatment of black persons than many ostensibly enlightened white political figures.

The death of Biko while in police custody, after a hunger strike lasting only seven days, raises grim questions about his handling while in custody and about the deaths of other black leaders in South Africa while in the hands of South African authorities. Biko was considered easily one of the three or four important black leaders in South Africa, especially important because of his youth and because young black student leaders in Soweto looked to him for leadership.

The attitude of white South African government officials after that death appalls one, very much in the way of some of the more outrageous comments from white political segregationist leaders in the 1950s and 1960s. Police Minister Jimmy Kruger spoke to a national party Nation Party Congress the day after the death was reported, and told an audience described as "snickering" by United Press International that the death of Biko "leaves me cold." It was the dead man's "democratic right to starve himself to death if he wanted," Kruger said.

The death of young Biko, a black leader apparently respected by a great many black and white persons who knew him, is tragic. The brutal, callous attitude of the South African government in response seems an ominous prophecy of even more tragic events to come.

Donald Woods
Escapes Banning

January 6, 1978

Those who love freedom can give a cheer this week for Donald Woods, the South African editor who fled his country after being placed under house arrest.

Authoritarian governments cannot endure serious criticism, and as a rule do not choose to endure it. The government of South Africa, quite aside from racial policies, has moved in a dictatorial way in recent months to crack down on free expression of opinion within South Africa. The *World*, the best-known daily newspaper with black staff and primarily black readership, was shut down altogether. Woods, the white newspaper editor of the *East London Daily Dispatch*, was "banned" at the same time.

The government gives no public reason in such cases. This "banning" meant that Woods was no longer permitted to practice journalism, that he was confined to his home, that he could not attend a meeting or even meet with a group of friends, that except for his immediate family he was barred from almost any other social contact at all.

Again, the government gives no reason in such cases; but the racist policies of the white regime in South Africa were clearly behind the actions. The *World*'s reporting of police-black conflicts in Soweto, the sprawling public housing project of more than a million black residents near Johannesburg, was just a little too vigorous for government observers. Woods, a well-known and respected editor for the past dozen years, had perhaps been more outspoken than any other white newspaper editor in South Africa in his criticism of the government's racial policies. So, it was easy to understand why the government sought to silence him by this "banning" for five years.

Woods had, among other things, been a personal friend of the late Steve Biko, the young black leader killed under mysterious circumstances while in the hands of the police, not the first black leader to die under such doubtful conditions. Woods was bold in his support of Biko and in his denunciation of the unexplained death.

A few days ago Woods disguised himself by dyeing his silvery hair and putting on a false mustache and then hitchhiking to the border and fleeing across to Lesotho. His family, wife Wendy and children, escaped by a different route.

Family was one of the reasons for fleeing. Some friendly soul in South Africa recently mailed two T-shirts to the Woods home, both with pictures of Steve Biko on them. Young Mary Woods, age five, put one of the T-shirts on; it had been saturated with acid and she was injured, but not permanently. But beyond his family's safety, Woods saw no chance that the South African government, as now constituted, would let him practice as a journalist again. He plans to go first to London and then to the United States where he will lecture and write.

Donald Woods is a brave man and a free man. The white minority government of South Africa, caught in its own formulas of racial discrimination, is neither as brave nor as free.

A Celebration,
Despite Haters

May 16, 1978

The haters are still out there, the genuine sick-minded ones, lest we forget. A celebration of Israel's thirtieth anniversary was held this past Sunday at the Jewish Community Center on Peachtree Street. The celebration was fine. Several thousand people attended and took part in honoring the third full decade of existence for a valiant nation.

But the celebration went forward after an attack by vandals, insensitive moral dullards who broke into the Jewish Community Center sometime Saturday afternoon or early evening, in an apparently conscious and deliberate effort to disrupt plans for that thirtieth celebration.

The vandals, probably more than one in light of the amount of destructive work committed, broke into the center sometime after 1 P.M. on Saturday. They had come and gone by 11 P.M., when a center official checked by and first noticed the damage.

Their shameful "work" began with breaking in through a wire-meshed glass in a sturdy door. Once inside, the criminals broke windows, painted Nazi swastikas on walls and floors, and defaced the faces on paintings and posters. The faces were burned out, perhaps with a blowtorch. There had been jars of food in the center, and these were broken and food smeared on walls and thrown on the ceiling in the kitchen area. Their work was thorough in its execution.

Mike Lainoff, assistant executive director of the center, observed that the message seemed clear, that it was not an effort to burn the center down, only one to commit destruction. Nothing of value was stolen, only broken. "It was very vicious, wanton nastiness," he said. That phrase will do nicely. It is accurate. The vandalism at the Jewish Community Center was indeed that, vicious, wanton nastiness.

It has only been a few years since a Jewish place of worship was bombed in Atlanta.

Those of goodwill quickly denounced that barbarous action, as it deserved denouncing. The raw, careless vandalism at the Jewish Community Center falls into the same category of evil. Sometimes we want to forget or turn our heads or just pretend that the haters are not really out there. But they really are. Moreover, they are capable of a deliberate destruction that springs from a twisted mind and a twisted spirit.

There is yet a cheerful note. Those planning the thirtieth anniversary celebration for Israel at the center quickly got to work and by Sunday had cleaned up most of the paint and food thrown about, patched up the vandalism as best they could.

The celebration was still what it should have been, a celebration of the spirit, in honor of a people and a young, vigorous nation whose history of three decades includes courage and commitment and compassion and valor. It was an open and proud celebration. The twisted spirits of the vandals rightly skulk in the dark. That's where they belong.

An Old Atlanta Visitor Turns Up

May 19, 1978

Atlanta has a distinguished visitor today, one who first came to this city on a visit of quite a different nature in 1960. The historical echoes in this instance are intriguing.

In 1960 a young school teacher named Kenneth David Kaunda came to visit an Atlantan, the late Dr. Martin Luther King, Jr. Kaunda (pronounced kah-OON-da) was just thirty-six, King was thirty-one. At the time Kaunda was teaching school in his native Zambia and he was also the unofficial leader of his countrymen in seeking independence. King was at just the beginning of the most effective part of his career as a national civil rights leader. The Montgomery boycott was behind him. But the March on Washington, the passage of civil rights legislation, the Nobel Peace Prize, these were all yet to come. King was well known enough already, though, for a young leader in Zambia to want to meet him and get to know him.

"I thought we should compare notes," Kaunda told a visitor last year, remembering that Atlanta visit of 1960. "We were

waging a non-violent struggle. He was waging the same kind
of non-violent struggle. It was helpful, very much so."

In 1964 Kaunda led his nation to independence from British colonial rule and became the first president of Zambia. Today, as the formal invitation to the ceremonies put it, "His
Excellency Doctor Kenneth D. Kaunda, President of the Republic of Zambia," will be honored by Mrs. Coretta King, the
widow of the man he once came to visit. Mrs. King and the directors of the King Center for Social Change will present
Kaunda with the Nonviolent Peace Prize, named for the man
with whom Kaunda once wanted to compare notes.

Now fifty-four, he is a remarkable man by any measure. He
is the son of a black Presbyterian missionary and he has successfully guided his young nation for the first decade and a
half of its existence. It has not been easy. Zambia is one of what
are called the "front-line" states, those African nations that
have common borders with South Africa and Rhodesia. He met
with President Carter and other officials in Washington this
week, before coming to Atlanta. That visit was actually scheduled for almost a full year ago, but border fighting between
Rhodesia and Zambia made him decide to delay his plans.
Kaunda has had problems with his nation's economy too,
problems not at all of his own making. Zambia is one of the
copper centers of the world, and the huge copper industry has
been its main source of export income. The world price of copper took a nose dive from a high in 1974 and has never quite
recovered.

Quite by coincidence as far as the timing, I was one of three
journalists invited to lunch with President Kaunda in Lusaka
exactly one year ago this week. He is an articulate, good-humored man, outgoing and friendly. He used to be a tennis
player, though now he has taken up golf. He neither drinks nor
smokes, but served his guests a good red wine with lunch and
gestured at the small pitcher by his plate. "I drink the white
wine," he said. It was buttermilk.

It is interesting to look back over my notes for that session
with Kaunda one year ago. He was pessimistic about the
chances of the American-British effort to work out a peaceful

transition of power in Rhodesia, a pessimism that seems amply justified by the events of the past year. He was more pessimistic about South Africa and the possibility of peaceful change there, and that view too has proved accurate in the last twelve months.

Prior to this week, Kaunda was last in Washington in April of 1975 and he had some strong comments about American failure to take any active role in the controversies involving Rhodesia and South Africa. His speech had a genuine impact and it changed the thinking apparently of both President Ford and Secretary of State Kissinger, who began moving in the direction urged by Kaunda.

"Three years ago, President Kaunda was here and made a strong speech that was embarrassing to his American host. Some said he should not have made it," President Carter observed during Kaunda's visit to the White House this week, adding, "Had we only listened to him . . . we could have avoided many serious mistakes. Zambia's policy has not changed, but our policy has changed."

Kenneth Kaunda is a rare man who combines idealism with a pragmatic sense of politics. His most praising words in relation to American policies referred to Carter's human rights theme, and he urged the president to "continue sounding the moral drums even louder." It is a pleasure to have him in Atlanta.

The Talmadge Dinosaur Era Is Fading

December 29, 1978[5]

Senator Herman Talmadge is somewhat of a political dinosaur, trying to survive on a political landscape littered with the bleached political bones of his fellow dinosaurs of yesteryear.

Sometimes Talmadge seems a little like one of those huge, ponderous dinosaurs, of the enormous body and weight and long neck, friendly enough, vegetarian even, not especially out for anyone's blood, but of such a size that no other creature would lightly seek a confrontation. Talmadge has dominated the politics of his home state in something of that fashion for fully three decades.

Recently, Talmadge has seemed more like the smaller but fiercer meat-eating dinosaurs, those of the squat body and

---

[5]Former Senator Herman Talmadge was twice elected governor of Georgia, serving from 1949 to 1955. He was first elected to the United States Senate in 1956 and reelected in 1962, 1968, and 1974. In 1980 Talmadge won a fiercely contested runoff for the Democratic Senate seat, then lost to Republican Mack Mattingly in the November election.

short neck and large, frightening teeth, ready for fight and eager for blood. He currently faces further investigation by the Senate Ethics Committee, possibly a censure hearing before the entire Senate, on charges of channeling campaign contributions into a secret bank account and of improperly drawing more than $37,000 in Senate expenses. A federal grand jury in Washington is considering the same charges and their legal implications.

Talmadge, in a dinosaur-like throwback to his political youth, labels the charges as fabrications of the bad old Atlanta newspapers—in his phrase, those "pernicious paragons of perfidy." It is not on record that Atlanta newspapers have any particular influence on the Senate Ethics Committee or federal grand juries in Washington, but Talmadge's father, the late Gov. Eugene Talmadge, specialized in running against the Atlanta newspapers and the senator may just be recalling the happy days of his political youth.

Dinosaurs faded from the scene years ago as the climate and other conditions around them changed, shifting from favorable to unfavorable. Most of the Southern senators around when Talmadge entered national politics faded long ago. Sen. Strom Thurmond of South Carolina, just reelected, is a notable exception. There are not many others.

Oh, Talmadge is not the kind of dinosaur that Sen. James Eastland of Mississippi became. Eastland chose in the end not to run because it was quite possible he would have been defeated, something once unthinkable, and because black voters would have supported almost anybody against him. Eastland made his overture to black voters much too late, and though some black leaders in Mississippi were sympathetic, there was not much market there for old segregationists. Talmadge is different. He made his overtures to black Georgia voters more than a decade ago. Calculated or not, it was with considerable political courage that Talmadge was the first statewide-elected figure in Georgia to accept a speaking engagement to the then all-black public school teacher association and another to Atlanta's Hungry Club.

Dinosaurs, though, are creatures who continue the same old habits, without adaptation, as the era changes. Talmadge may or may not face serious legal problems or censure from the Senate. It is his pattern of old habits, especially with money, that will trouble him most if he runs for reelection in 1980, as he has said he would. This is the post-Watergate time, the time after the Imperial Presidency, and yes, the time after the Imperial Congress.

Sen. Talmadge has many vigorous defenders. Few, however, are under fifty years old. A great many voters under forty have only a vague sense of Talmadge as a public figure at all; they were toddlers or not born when the Talmadge Tyrannosaurus Rex cut political teeth. How many of these younger voters will understand a U. S. senator who seemingly never wanted for cash and yet never cashed a check for cash for years and years? Or will think it routine that car dealers gave the senator cars for his use at no charge over the years? Or can understand easily that his ex-wife, Betty, could testify to the Senate Ethics Committee that the senator gave her a "considerable amount" of cash over the years, including presumably some of those years when the senator was not cashing checks? Or understand how it is exactly that the senator could not pay taxes on a $756,241 gross profit on a sale of land in Cobb County, letting wife Betty pay the capital-gains tax, then claiming later (successfully in court) that the land and money were his all along? Or not wonder why it is that a United States senator should be reaping such profit on any basis for a speculative land investment just off a federal interstate highway? Or will not question the propriety of Georgia's senior senator, who says he is a multimillionaire, accepting frequent cash gifts from supporters wherever he goes?

Dinosaurs last a long time, often. The climate changes, their political ice age comes. Few survive.

The Friends
of Herman Talmadge
Prevailed at Last

February 7, 1979

In the end, it was the old friends of Sen. Herman Talmadge, those who cared more about his health than his politics, who prevailed.

Some of the stories were not new, stories of serious drinking bouts by the Georgia senator, tales of his dropping out for days at a time without a sober breath. The stories have been around for years, even decades. One Washington friend said that until fairly recently the pattern had been for Talmadge to remain reasonably sober most of the time, for maybe two or three months at a time, and then maybe get knee-walking drunk for two or three days.

That pattern changed in recent months, the friend said, as the intervals between those bad periods got shorter and shorter. Talmadge has in the last couple of years lost one of his sons, been through a bitter divorce battle, and currently faces serious probes of his handling of Senate and of campaign funds by the Senate Ethics Committee and by a federal grand jury in Washington. He had some reason to take a drink, both friends and staff believed, but not to the extent that his drinking finally reached.

There were some terrible stories, sad and unhappy stories. One was of Talmadge sitting alone in an office, the curtains drawn, the room almost dark, talking with an old friend, but as if he were, well, not drunk, but just not operating in the real world. A group of Florida farmers called on Talmadge one morning in his role as chairman of the Senate Agricultural Committee. Maybe they didn't like what they heard from the senator, but in any case, a Florida newspaper did a story quoting a majority of the farmer delegation who said that they believed Talmadge had been skunk drunk in the middle of the morning. There were other recent stories, like the one of a couple of weeks ago, that Talmadge was drunk and staggering on the opening day of the new Senate, the day when senators were sworn in. Maybe he was ill, one sympathetic senator commented.

In the end it was those who cared more about Talmadge the man than Talmadge the politician who prevailed. There was a split, on his staff and among his friends, when Talmadge was admitted to the Naval Medical Center at Bethesda, Maryland, on 22 January, a Monday. That was just one week after his colleagues in the Senate, though they would not say it publicly, had observed Talmadge in such uncertain shape on the day of the swearing-in. Some Talmadge boosters wanted to dodge the drinking issue, though they understood by then that nobody could drink that much for long and live. Others insisted that this wasn't politics any more, that the 1980 reelection campaign was something else; what they worried about was whether the senator would still be alive in 1980 unless drastic action were taken. So then, in the end Talmadge's own office announced that he was being admitted to the hospital for "exhaustion, fatigue and alcohol abuse."

Talmadge did not stay there long. On Thursday, he was moved at his own request to the Navy alcoholism treatment center in Long Beach, California. The doctors recommended it, but that was probably not the crucial factor.

A small group of Talmadge's oldest friends in the Congress paid a visit to him while he was still in the Maryland hospital. Talmadge has a reputation as a loner, not one to run much with a crowd, but these were his oldest and best friends in the United States Congress. His fellow senator from Georgia, Sam Nunn, was there. So were Sen. John Stennis of Mississippi, Sen. Russell Long of Louisiana, and Congressman Ronald "Bo" Ginn of Georgia (who once worked as an aide for Talmadge).

They spoke bluntly to Georgia's senior senator. We are your friends, they said, probably the best friends you have in Washington. We are on your side, we want to help you lick this thing, but you are at a point that goes way beyond politics. Either you kick the bottle or you are going to die, they said, either you take yourself in hand or just forget about politics and everything else.

There was no argument, curiously. Talmadge looked at the group and, one of those there said later, his only real question was about his committee work. He looked over at Russell Long, perhaps his closest personal friend in the Senate, and asked if Long would be in a position to handle Talmadge committee commitments while Talmadge was away. Long readily promised that he would.

Some around Talmadge are worried more about his politics than his health, about his 1980 reelection bid, even about their own jobs on his staff. Talmadge understood, though, that those visiting him in the Bethesda hospital were there only as his friends, willing to help him in his politics too, but worried first of all about Herman Talmadge—their friend, a man who has to come to grips with himself or die.

Preserving
Christian Silence
on Hungry Children

March 8, 1979

Poor people don't have much lobbying influence. They never have. The current, sorry session of the Georgia General Assembly offers an illustration of this.

Put it down, friends, though most of you understand it already. The major banks, the big utilities, the big landowners, most anybody with big bucks, all have their lobbyists and lawyers walking the corridors of the state capitol to exert self-serving influence on pending legislation. Oh, throw in newspapers too, of course. Publishers and editors are perfectly capable of wrapping themselves in the banner of the First Amendment and raising cain on whatever side of an issue they favor. We like to think, at its best, that this works for a free press in a free society, but the element of self-interest is there often enough.

Schoolteachers have gotten to be pretty good lobbyists too. They marched on the state capitol the other day and in the end stampeded the Georgia House to increase their proposed raises substantially.

The poor are not good at this process, though. They tend often to be hungry, for one thing. That makes it a little harder to focus your mind on lobbying your friendly neighborhood legislator. They tend also to be disadvantaged in other ways: not likely to dress well, often not likely really to understand how the legislature works at all, not the sort of people you tend to see over at the state capitol making their views known.

The poor in Georgia also tend to be children. There are 150,000 of them presently receiving benefits from the Aid to Families with Dependent Children program. That's three out of four of the people receiving AFDC benefits. Disadvantaged children don't really make good lobbyists. They understand about being hungry some days, not living very happily; they don't understand much about influencing lawmakers.

Governor George Busbee, to his great credit, recommended a thirty percent increase in the AFDC benefits. The benefits are pitifully small at present. The state currently pays only $148 in welfare benefits for a family of four. That's not much, and you start with such a low base that even a thirty percent boost isn't anything to write home about. Busbee did well in his recommendation, though, understanding that Georgia is the forty-sixth state in the nation in providing care for the poor.

The Georgia House, in its wisdom, gutted this recommendation. The House voted a 7.7 percent increase in the supplemental budget, the one holding just until June 30. They voted then only to continue that 7.7 percent boost in the new fiscal year's budget.

There is at least one organized group trying to promote support for the children, calling itself Christians Against Hunger in Georgia. There are some prominent members of the Georgia House who call themselves great Christians (defined so in part because they do not drink or smoke) who vote against the children without blinking an eye. A former House member, prominent too in his time, observed once that he never had believed this notion that Christians were people who went around in sackcloth and ashes, that he thought being a Christian meant somebody who cared for his fellow man.

There are a lot of Sunday Christians around who aren't much heard from during the week. There are a number of clergymen, too, who take an interest in a rather narrow range of public issues. Let a bingo bill or a liquor bill come down the pike and they write letters to their legislators. Let come the issue of the welfare benefits that so directly and vitally affect the lives of 150,000 children, and these same clergymen are strangely silent.

On the Southern Way of Life in Pierce County

April 11, 1979

The blatant racism of Pierce County Superior Court Judge Elie L. Holton disgraces this state. It is an outrage in this day and time that an attorney, Millard Farmer, can be jailed for contempt of court when his single crime was to insist that his client, a black man, be addressed in court with the same ordinary courtesy routinely used with white men and women.

Farmer objected when the district attorney persisted in calling his client, George Street, only by the client's first name. The phrase, Mister Street, was too much for the prosecutor to handle. Yet the same prosecutor found it easy enough to address any white man in the court as Mister. Judge Holton, incredibly, upheld this leftover racism of a day that is past and cited Farmer on two counts of contempt of court for objecting.

What amazes one is that this simple brand of racism could still exist in any courtroom in Georgia, let alone a state superior court, where the most serious kinds of cases are tried.

The South and the nation have gone through a sea change with the civil rights revolution of the last two decades. Those of us who have lived through it understand that we have come a long way and yet understand too that on many fronts there is a long way to go. Segregation laws in the South were only part of the picture. There were patterns of segregation too, some subtle and some not so subtle. One was the habit of addressing a black man, an adult, by his first name only, as one might address a child. The use of the word Mister was reserved for white men.

There were, without question, many whites and blacks who accepted such customs almost innocently, without thinking too much about them. That was still possible only a few years ago. It is not possible to imagine such things being accepted in unthinking fashion today, frankly. It is not possible to imagine a district attorney in any superior court in Georgia refusing to call a black man Mister without understanding that this was a form of racial discrimination, a kind of patronizing racial slur. It is not possible to imagine a superior court judge in Georgia so totally unconscious of the last two decades of American history that he fails to understand that there is racial discrimination in the refusal to offer the same courtesy of address to a black person as to a white person.

Farmer's client, George Street, came out all right in the court proceeding, in a sense. He had been sentenced to death for murder. A higher court raised the question of whether Street had properly been given a death sentence and ordered a new jury to consider that issue alone; the jury gave Street a life sentence rather than the death penalty. Farmer will come out all right, too. He is a fairly abrasive fellow, one who crusades against the death penalty. It is easy to imagine Farmer irritating a district attorney or a judge. But his time in jail in Pierce County can properly be worn as a badge of honor. His guilt lies in speaking too determinedly for justice, in pressing too strongly for an end to a brand of racism that has no place in a Georgia courtroom.

We have come a long way in this state in ending the racial discriminations of the past. Surely, though, the taint of racism in the administration of justice is a serious matter indeed. One group of fifteen Georgia lawyers petitioned the Superior Court of Pierce County in Farmer's behalf, declaring their belief that

an attorney *should* object to "officially condoned manifestations of racism and inequality in the courtroom," even asking
permission to serve Farmer's jail sentence in his place. Those
attorneys represent the future, and are part of the slow, steady
progress towards an era without racial discrimination. Judge
Holton's ruling upholding racism in his courtroom relates to
something else, a touch of the dead hand of a shabby past, the
time when discrimination was cherished by many as the
Southern way of life.

On the *Brown* Decision After Twenty-five Years

May 17, 1979

One survey of college students recently indicated that the phrase, *Brown vs. Board of Education*, had meaning only to about one in ten and yet that decision was a major part of a significant reshaping of American society.

That was the landmark school desegregation decision, made exactly twenty-five years ago, a controversial decision of the United States Supreme Court, handed down by what its critics soon called the "nine old men" on that high court.

In retrospect, the first thing that occurs to me was how little that decision actually meant in any immediate terms. That is, it was a bombshell and it would mean great change in the South and the nation. But there was literally a period of about a year or so when nothing changed much at all. Many Southern political figures kept fairly quiet about the implications of the decision. Some even voiced a tentative belief that the South would move reasonably and promptly to comply with the law.

The demagogues came quickly enough, of course. There were eventually the Southern senators and governors and lesser lights by the score and more who denounced the Supreme Court for daring to suggest that segregated public schools were unfair and unequal, and that black Americans were just as entitled as white Americans to equal educational opportunities.

Attorney General Griffin Bell reflected on that time in comments in a special *Atlanta Constitution* report published this week on the twenty-fifth anniversary of the *Brown* decision. Bell served on the Fifth Circuit U. S. Court of Appeals for fifteen years and he personally dealt with 141 school desegregation rulings. He has had some reason to reflect on that part of our history.

The Brown suit, he observed the other day, sought several remedies, including "one that no American today would think of denying, that was 'Let our children go to the school nearest their home, don't make us walk by a white school to get to a black school, just let us go to the schoolhouse nearest our home.' " If the U. S. Supreme Court had not added to its phrase "with all deliberate speed," Bell reflected that within ninety days every single student in every school system would have been permitted to go to the school nearest home, then "it would have been all over with, in my judgment."

Bell adds that he understands this is Monday-morning quarterbacking, and my own belief is that the process of change could never have come quite that easily. The strong forces in favor of preserving the status quo of a segregated system mobilized pretty quickly. Southern governors and legislators passed packages of laws aimed at circumventing the U. S. Supreme Court rulings. Lower federal courts were swamped with lawsuits from school boards and local governments aimed at delaying the process of school desegregation as much as possible. Those in the federal government favoring desegregation were for a long while sympathetic to the notion that it would take time. The very "best people" in the white community did some of the worst things. Don't ever believe the redneck types with cruel eyes were the ones who fought for segregation. They were lawyers who belonged to the best private clubs and accepted huge fees to lose anti-school-desegregation lawsuits all the way to the U. S. Supreme Court. They were the school and college officials who took the witness stand in federal courts and lied under oath, insisting that their institutional policies were really not designed to maintain segregation. They were the ministers who preached in their churches on Sunday—oh, sometimes very subtly—that racism was the will of God.

But there were the courageous ones too, white and black, who in the end helped make the *Brown* decision part of a society committed to moving away from the racism of the past. There is still a way to go, though.

Dr. King
Changed America
for the Better

January 15, 1980[6]

He changed this country, measurably and for the better, and we will get around to making his birthday a national holiday. His birthday falls today. Dr. Martin Luther King, Jr. would have been fifty-one years old on this day. He was not given much time. There are a goodly number of people of significance whose achievements were still unwritten at age fifty-one. That age probably seems ancient to teenagers, but it seems younger and younger to those of us on the other side of age forty. In any case, the history books recount the varied contributions of those whose careers were only beginning to flourish in their 50s or 60s.

But, again, King did not have much time. He was shot down in Memphis even before he reached age forty. He was thirty-nine when the assassin's bullet sought him out on that motel balcony.

----

[6]The late Dr. King's birthday was indeed declared a national holiday by the United States Congress in late 1983.

Yet he changed this country, and for the better. The times were ripe, of course. There had been court decisions chipping away at the patterns and customs of racial segregation for a couple of decades by the time Martin King became a national figure. He became, however, the single national figure who best articulated the aspirations of black Americans who sought the most fundamental of freedoms, simply to be treated equally as citizens despite a difference in the color of their skin.

There is a fair argument that King meant more to white Americans than to black. He lived and he understood the frustrations of those who shared his ethnic background. He voiced their hopes, their dreams. No one ever thundered forth those basics more eloquently than King, or more personally, as when he dared to hope that his children would be judged in this nation by their character rather than their color. His message, though, for white Americans was equally deep-set, etched in the racial wrongs of two centuries plus. King spoke to the heart and conscience of white Americans. He made eyes see and perceive. He made hearts understand what it was like to be treated unfairly and unjustly because of the accident of skin color. King, in the most profound sense, liberated white Americans fully as much as he helped liberate black Americans.

King was criticized, cursed, despised as a troublemaker and a radical, and finally shot down in Memphis by a bullet propelled as much by hatred as by gunpowder. Yet withal, and this is part of his legacy too, he never yielded to hatred himself. He felt the frustrations of his era but he resisted the bitterness that might have crippled him, even as hatred and bitterness crippled others, white and black. He put his trust in God, and he put his trust in the potential goodness in the hearts of people, no matter how difficult at times it was to discern that goodness.

His legacy lives and will live as long as the nation survives, as long as the memories of, say, a Thomas Jefferson or an Abraham Lincoln stay with us. Today is not a bad day, King's birthday, to reflect that one of this nation's genuine heroes came from Atlanta and Georgia.

On the Immoral Moral Majority

February 13, 1981

The trouble with the Moral Majority is that its members are as a rule not necessarily moral and, the good Lord willing, as yet a long way from a majority.

Their morality consists mainly of trying to impose on everyone else their own sense of values, regardless of other people's values or of the pluralism of our society. They don't much like Jews, aren't much on any minority, and they are bigoted. Bigotry by definition refers to those who are intolerant of any beliefs other than their own; that describes the Moral Majority crowd.

There are nasty little examples in our own state of Georgia. One of the most vicious political campaigns in recent memory was in DeKalb County last fall when an avowed candidate of the Moral Majority ran against Rep. Eleanor Richardson. It was an ugly campaign. Mrs. Richardson has supported the Equal Rights Amendment and other progressive measures under the gold dome of the state capitol. That amounts to sinful doings in the eyes of the MM crowd.

Campaign literature was distributed against Rep. Richardson asserting that she favored lesbianism, prostitution, and other assorted evil doings. The irony of this particular shabby little campaign is that Mrs. Richardson is known to a host of people for what she is—an attractive, intelligent woman interested in community affairs who in many ways has lived a rather traditional life-style. She is a mother and a grandmother married to the same fellow for a lot of years and has about as much in common with the scurrilous campaign attack on her character as the Rev. Jerry Falwell has with the Apostle Paul.

The Rev. Falwell, by the way, is the Founding Father, so to speak, of the Moral Majority. He believes in Sin, as defined by the Rev. Falwell. He believes in Christianity, as defined by the Rev. Falwell. He believes in goodness, as defined by the Rev. Falwell. Everyone else is out of step; you are moral in the Rev. Falwell's terms or you are full of evil and sin and rightly damned to hell.

He is a dangerous man, not because he holds strong beliefs as he has every right to do, but because he wants to impose his beliefs on everyone else. He shares that trait with Adolf Hitler, and he also shares Hitler's belief that somehow history and destiny are on his side, that he (Falwell) is the wave of the future.

Some manifestations of the Moral Majority are simply funny (the campaign against Rep. Richardson was not). In Maryland the friendly folk at MM launched a campaign against X-rated cookies. I know, I know, but it is true. A bakery—heaven knows why exactly, except that the good old free-enterprise system is at work—decided to market cookies described by the *Wall Street Journal* as "anatomically explicit gingerbread men and women." The MM folk brought suit, outraged at the thought of those terrible cookies falling into the wrong hands. The suit was dropped after it got almost laughed out of court; a member of the state legislature asked the legislative counsel's office to draw up a proposed law, the Pornographic Cookie Control Act of 1981.

There are, no doubt, people who consider themselves highly moral and part of a moral majority. More power to them as long as they keep to one side of bigotry.

Stokely Carmichael's Old Brand of Racist Rhetoric

March 23, 1981

Stokely Carmichael, aging civil rights activist of the 1960s, was back in Atlanta last week preaching racial hate to anyone who would listen.

Carmichael is a sad case in a way. He was young, black, intelligent, and articulate in the early 1960s, when those traits moved him quickly into a position of leadership within the civil rights movement. He became head of the Student Nonviolent Coordinating Committee (SNCC) in 1966 and he was often quoted as a national figure. Somehow he may be a psychological casualty of those times. One story had it that he turned exceedingly bitter after a friend in the civil rights movement, a white clergyman, was shot down and killed for no good reason other than the preaching of racial fairness and equality.

Carmichael forgot the message preached by his friend, however. He turned instead to racial hate. That was the day of the slogan of "Black Power." Carmichael and others took the line that black people must work hard to help themselves—fine so far—but they also claimed that all white people were evil, that white Americans would never really live up even to the civil rights laws already passed, and certainly never really treat black Americans as first-class citizens.

That was a lie. It was a lie then and it is still a lie now. There were white Americans who marched and who legislated and who, yes, gave up their lives in order that Carmichael and other black American citizens might have a fair chance at the American dream.

Carmichael took a racist twist, fully as racist as the Ku Klux Klan. He purged SNCC of whites, some of whom had credentials fully as good as those of Stokely Carmichael in the civil rights movement. He left the country eventually, and for the past few years has lived in Africa. But his message last week in Atlanta had not changed from the 1960s. It was a message of racism and hate and dangerous, demagogic nonsense. Maybe dangerous is almost too complimentary a word, because Atlanta has come a long way past Carmichael's brand of inflammatory rhetoric.

Atlanta's cases of the slain and missing children will not be solved by Atlanta police, proclaimed Carmichael, because the Atlanta police department is "racist to the core."

Is the joker serious? It may have escaped Carmichael during his overseas travels, but Atlanta is one of those communities where the civil rights revolution produced both political and economic power for black Americans. Oh, we have our differences. But the fabric of the community is strong enough that black and white public officials and citizens are able to disagree and argue on some things, yet never question in most cases whether we are one community and whether most of us care deeply about our city and people. We care about our children, too. Carmichael does not. He is willing to accept the deaths of Atlanta's youngsters in order to deal in racist rhetoric.

Is the fellow serious? A racist police department in Atlanta when the city has a black mayor, a black public safety commissioner, and a black police chief? Not to mention a substantial number of white and black police officers at all levels who figured out a while ago that good law enforcement is not a matter of race but of competence and ability and caring.

Stokely Carmichael is a sour, fading voice from another decade. It was a voice of racism and hate then. It still is today. Atlantans, black and white, have little interest in the divisive racist rhetoric of the past.

Ol' Hosea
Had a Pretty
Fair Week

May 7, 1981

The Right Rev. Rep. Hosea has had a pretty fair week so far. First of all, a judge said that he would not have to go to jail, at least not right away. Second, ol' Hosea will be meeting today with President Ronald Reagan to talk about more majestic things. Both are interesting turns of the world.

The judge had to take a hard look at Rep. Williams's driving record, a chore roughly equivalent to that old saw about making laws and making sausages: don't ever look at the process of either too carefully or it might upset you.

Rep. Williams was still on probation on a conviction of being a habitual offender, which basically means you do a lot of illegal things while driving and keep on driving after the authorities tell you to quit. Then, he was caught again for driving in doubtful circumstances and for allegedly fleeing the scene of an accident. The jury thought there was no "allegedly" to it, deciding that ol' Hosea was guilty as charged; he will appeal to all possible high courts. The judge had to decide whether to revoke the Georgia solon's probation on the spot or let the appeals process work its way through. The judge, probably quite reasonably, said he would let Rep. Williams have his chance in the appeals process and revoke the probation only if the initial conviction on the more recent charge is upheld.

To the White House? Why not? Ol' Hosea rolled the dice last fall, choosing to support Reagan for president when there were just not very many black faces out there on the Reagan side. The Rev. Ralph David Abernathy of Atlanta and Charles Evers of Mississippi were among the other few. Ol' Hosea will explain to you about how black folk have been trying to get off welfare for years and how Reagan economics will help us all. Ah well, don't fault him for that; a considerable number of white politicos have done twists and turns of an equally stunning nature.

Indeed, I must say I rise to join my colleague Frederick Allen, chief political writer for the *Atlanta Constitution*, who wrote a good column about Hosea Williams the other day. The gist of the Allen column was that it is too easy to dismiss this battered old rabble-rouser, veteran of hundreds of marches and demonstrations in the civil rights movement. He is a veteran in more ways than one, a man who got himself shot up pretty badly in World War II fighting for this country. That was one of the reasons that it did not seem quite right to Hosea, when he came home again, to believe in a system in which black Americans were by definition inferior. There are most curious connections in this world. Hosea, just out of uniform, went home to Bainbridge and was soon elected head of the black American Legion chapter; Cheney Griffin, brother of former Gov. Marvin Griffin, was just home from the war, too, and at the same time became head of the white American Legion. They became friends and Griffin helped pay Rep. Williams's way through Morris Brown College.

Williams had it made after that, in a way: he became a chemist, a professional man, an affluent middle-class black in Savannah with a good job who frankly did not have to worry much about the direct effect of segregation on him personally. But he gave that up to throw himself into the civil rights movement with an almost incredible energy, intelligence, compelling rhetoric, and verve. He is a peacemaker, too, believe it or not; the fingers on both hands would not count the times that Hosea Williams has walked into a potentially violent situation and tried to soothe people, tried to keep folk from getting hurt.

Pretty good case, as my colleague Mr. Allen put it, that Hosea does not belong behind the wheel of a car. I'm not sure that it is so clear that he should go to jail. Or, try it another way. It would be interesting to have Hosea Williams at Reidsville for a year; there would be a new organization of prison inmates within a couple of months, and I will offer five-to-one odds that I can tell you the name of its chief spokesman right now.

Let Us Mourn
for What We Did
to Jerry Banks

May 26, 1981[7]

Let us now mourn Jerry Banks, dead by his own hand. Let us mourn for what we did to him. Let us mourn, too, his wife, Virginia, shot down by her own husband at age twenty-seven. Let us mourn especially the children of this marriage.

There are three orphans now. Jerry, Jr. is eleven, Elbert is eight, and the youngest, Felicia Ann, is seven. Felicia was born in 1974, the same year when we railroaded Jerry Banks into jail for a double murder he did not commit.

Let us mourn for ourselves. We are responsible, you and I, for the way the system of justice operates in the state of Georgia; when it operates to the total injustice of tearing one individual's life and family apart, we are responsible.

We are responsible for Jerry Banks and his six years on Death Row, six years that must have been almost incredibly de-

---

[7]Members of the Georgia Supreme Court deserve high praise for their pursuit of justice in this case, as do the attorneys who persisted in appealing the two convictions. The local lawyers involved functioned indeed as the conscience of their community.

spairing because he knew with utter certainty in his own mind and heart that he had not committed any crime, that somehow the system of justice itself had gone wrong and he did not quite know what an individual could do about it. Oh, we are responsible.

We know, too, enough about the case now not to think of turning our heads, though that would certainly be more comfortable and more convenient.

Convenient? Nice word in this case. Jerry Banks was the convenient black man. Convenient in that the local law could grab him as a target of opportunity, and accuse him of a double murder, and count on his confusion and on the kind of railroad-job court trial that ought to embarrass every lawyer in this state. Case solved.

Consider what happened to Jerry Banks, briefly. You want to know more? Write me, I'll send you the information just on those things not disputed at all. Banks may have committed a greater sin than most of us; he may have tried to be a good citizen in the kind of circumstance that would make most folk panic. He was out hunting one day, came upon two people in a wooded section of Henry County, both dead, both white, one the bandleader at Jonesboro High, the other a former student. This next little bit is undisputed: Jerry Banks headed for the nearest highway, flagged down a motorist, and asked the driver to call the sheriff so that he, Banks, could wait and show the law enforcement people where the bodies were.

Later, the sheriff's office said that shotgun shells found near the scene came from Banks's own shotgun. Don't let me bore you with all the evidence that eventually surfaced, or about a local lawman who had a reputation for faking evidence, or of evidence offered by good Henry County citizens that was suppressed. No, let me only offer the view of the Georgia Supreme Court, which could tell that something smelled to high heaven in this case and twice tossed out a murder conviction and ordered a new trial, the last time saying that there was enough new evidence to raise the question as to whether Jerry Banks ever had received a fair trial. It was after that second high court expressed its view that the local prosecution concluded that the flimsy evidence that had railroaded Banks in the first place needed no further remodeling; he was released.

There was a point after Banks had been on Death Row, for a crime he never committed, when he despaired to his lawyers and asked them to end the appeals, saying that he wanted to go on and die in the electric chair. The process of it all was too painful. He changed his mind, and could say later after his release, "I couldn't sit here and tell you that I believe in God and say that I'm angry at anybody. We're all human. We all make mistakes."

The release came, let it be noted, not because you and I made the criminal justice system function very well. Banks was railroaded to Death Row as the convenient black man. We gave him in defense two incompetent lawyers in a row, one later disbarred. If there were any redeeming features, it was only in the people who came to care about such a colossal injustice: the local lawyers (white, by the way) who raged and sweated and spent untold hours of unpaid time in pursuing the case, and in the perceptive judgments made by the Georgia Supreme Court.

So he became free and lived happily forever. Freed in December of last year, helped by some to find work, wanting to start again; his wife had suffered, Lord knows how much, during the Death Row time. Somehow he and she could not make it work again as a family. She wanted a divorce, he resisted; for he seemed to feel that the notion of his family had been the only thing holding him together in the six years we kept him on Death Row. He killed himself and his wife.

The children, the three young Banks children, are innocent, whatever else. The attorneys who spent so much time saving him, whose hearts broke when his new freedom ended in violence and death, are trying now to look after the children.

How a New
Congressman
Got Elected

July 26, 1981 *

Congressman Wayne Dowdy was strolling one sunny afternoon last week from the Capitol building in Washington over to the Longworth office building, where his new offices are on the sixth floor.

It was interesting to note that several people seemed to recognize him and go out of their way to speak, interesting because Dowdy is hardly an old Washington hand. It is barely three weeks now since the thirty-seven-year-old mayor of McComb, Mississippi, became the newest member of the United States House, winning the July 7th special election in a narrow upset victory.

Now, special elections to fill House congressional seats are not unusual. Atlanta Congressman Wyche Fowler first won his present seat in a special election. There are almost always a couple pending somewhere in the country, two at least in the

---

*This essay originally appeared in the Sunday *Atlanta Journal and Constitution*.

next several weeks. Dowdy will not remain the brand-spanking newest member of Congress for long.

Yet he is recognized because in his case both the national Republican and national Democratic parties want to read national significance in this special election (the Republicans far less so, of course, since Dowdy's victory, but with interest enough earlier to warrant President Ronald Reagan's personal telephone call to wish the Republican candidate well and for the Republican party to plow an estimated $300,000 into the election).

It started out as a kind of messy election. This is the district that was represented by Rep. Jon Hinson, the congressman who resigned after being arrested on homosexual charges in a men's room in a congressional office building.

Yet the Republicans had seemingly every reason to feel great confidence in the outcome. This district has been represented by a Republican congressman for the last nine years. It was held earlier by Rep. Thad Cochran, who went on to be elected senator from Mississippi.

Indeed, the first balloting was almost totally cheerful for the Republican candidate, Liles Williams, who broke forty percent in a field of several candidates, with Dowdy a not-so-close second. The runoff was something else. Dowdy happens to be white, but he credits the huge turnout of black voters in the runoff for his victory.

It was a rough runoff campaign. The Republicans used pictures in campaign material of Dowdy, Mississippi black leader Aaron Henry, and House Speaker Tip O'Neill. Dowdy campaigned hard among rural and black voters especially and his campaign ran get-out-to-vote radio ads on stations with mostly black audiences.

Dowdy, incidentally, downplays the great national significance of his victory, saying he wants to represent the district well. But there is a national import, not necessarily as any sort of referendum on Reagan economic policies or as any reaffirmation of the Democratic party, but more along the line of suggesting that the Voting Rights Act has somewhat of a different impact than many believed.

That is, Dowdy's opponents believed that general Democratic support of that legislation would hurt a Democratic candidate. Dowdy's campaign pushed the theme that his Republican opponent opposed the Voting Rights Act. The outcome? Black voters cared about the issue in great numbers, white voters apparently did not.

Two Good
Old Boys
from Dooly

October 26, 1981

Two good old boys from Dooly County got together for a brief visit the other evening, including remembering when they used to live up the street from each other. Some would say that neither one has done a lick of honest work in years; some might even suggest that each had chosen a slightly less than honorable profession.

One wandered away from Vienna as a young man and ended up practicing law in Albany. The other's career took an even worse twist, taking him to the badlands of Washington, where he is forced to deal on a regular basis with politicians and journalists. The first fellow, Gov. George Dekle Busbee, couldn't stay long to visit the other evening. He had to go make a speech of his own, no doubt in support of the Equal Rights Amendment. The second, Eugene H. Methvin, was the speaker of the evening at the Atlanta Lawyers Club.

Now, Methvin grew up as an ink-stained wretch in Vienna, where his mother and father ran the *Vienna News*; most of us who come to such a fate have to work over a period of time at getting there. He worked once on this newspaper, and his jour-

nalistic career took him after a time to Washington, where he
is now a senior editor of the *Reader's Digest* in its Washington
office.

Methvin has kept alive a rather keen sense of his Georgia
ties and Georgia history. He found it pretty remarkable, he
said, that a Georgia Tech graduate could end up walking on
the back side of the moon. But he found just as remarkable the
events that had shaped the political landscape in his native
state in the past few years.

They might have locked him up a few years ago, he suggested, if he had tried to tell anybody that a computer salesman from Indiana would defeat Sen. Herman Talmadge for a
United States Senate seat. Or if he had tried to sell the notion
that a peanut farmer from a Georgia town smaller than Vienna would run for president of the United States and make it
to the White House. Or, fully as incredible, if he had tried to tell
them that an aging Hollywood actor would then run against
the Georgia peanut farmer and win the presidency. It has been
a remarkable period of time for Georgians and Americans, and
we sometimes forget the depth and breadth of the changes.

Methvin is proud of his newspapering parents, with good
reason. They ran a small county newspaper with courage and
a sense of justice when such things were not easy in the South.
Perhaps such things are never easy; but in the South, on the
racial front, the time of the 1930s was an especially difficult
time.

A black man in Dooly County was arrested after cursing
and threatening the sheriff. The sheriff's story after the arrest
was that he was trying to take his prisoner to another county
jail for safety's sake when masked men stopped him and took
his prisoner; the prisoner's body was soon found swinging
from a tree.

As the younger Methvin wrote about it later, that was a
time when lynching was considered a perfectly acceptable
method of race relations. His parents did not suffer such happenings gladly, even though his father was told rather
strongly that he'd better "soft-pedal" the story. Instead, the *Vienna News* ran a front-page editorial declaring of the mob vio-

lence, "Each man who had a part in it is a cold-blooded murderer, since no one can deny that 'who hunts with the pack is responsible for the kill.' " The editorial ended with this plea: "Let's make it unhealthy for such gangs to operate in Dooly."

Well, for a good while the editor had to carry a pistol for protection, but Gene Methvin's parents helped make that plea come true. He's proud of them and has good reason to be. They helped bring us where we are.

On Reliving
That Monkey Trial
in Tennessee

December 21, 1981

They called it the "Monkey Trial" more than half a century ago when an obscure Tennessee public school teacher a bit inadvertently gave his name to the Scopes trial.

The school teacher, even then, seemed a rather unprepossessing fellow to create so much stir. He insisted on teaching Darwin's theories of evolution in his high school science class; his sin, and it was certainly called a sin by Christian fundamentalists, was to teach the scientific theory that human beings had evolved over the millions of years; that men and women might indeed have developed gradually from more basic life forms; that indeed we as human beings might number monkeys (or related animals) among our ancestors in the long scheme of evolution.

Oh, the Christian fundamentalists were having none of that, not of the monkey talk, or even the very suggestion that the Earth might have existed for millions of years. There were some alleged biblical scholars who asserted with conviction that God had created the Earth and universe at exactly such and so a day and hour, only a few thousand years ago.

The trial brought out the titans of the time, and about as much press coverage as any trial of the era. Clarence Darrow, the best-known criminal lawyer of his time, defended the school teacher. William Jennings Bryan, a former candidate for president and former secretary of state, denounced the teacher and such godless beliefs.

Darrow won, really. The school teacher was convicted, but only after most people involved had become embarrassed over the whole case. The court imposed the most minimal fine and was glad the case was over; Bryan fell ill and died only a short time later.

What is incredible is that right now, in 1981, some fifty-six years later, we are going through in this country the very repeat of that famous Scopes trial. The most recent version finished up in Arkansas only last week, a test of that state's new law on what is now called "creation science," a law that, in effect, requires the public schools to teach a rather conservative Christian view of God and creation, along with teaching any scientific theories about evolution.

The nine-day trial finished in Little Rock last week. The judge said it would be at least this week sometime before the ruling. A similar trial on a similar law is coming up shortly in Louisiana. It is remarkable, because the argument really has not changed since the 1920s.

Science cannot pretend to be religion, nor should religion pretend to be science. Every American is entitled in our free system to believe in God and religion in whatever fashion strikes his or her soul most compellingly. No American is entitled to impose a particular religious view on youngsters in public schools, and that is exactly what these "creation science" laws are all about, the effort to enforce a religious view.

There was a Canadian historian called as one witness in the Arkansas case, Michael Ruse, who observed that science in general is explanatory, testable and tentative, and yet religious beliefs are none of these.

That is a good summary. Religion touches the heart and soul and innermost being. Maybe it is in a profound sense more important than any science. But it is not science. Scientific theories are, in fact, subject to testing and examining and confirming (or disproving) on the basis of existing evidence and theory. Religion is not based on theory and evidence and facts, but rather on belief and commitment and inner vision. That distinction really was clear at the Scopes trial in the 1920s. It still is.

Trial Ends
Long Trauma
in Atlanta

March 1, 1982

The most bizarre and compelling murder case in Atlanta history reached a resolution Saturday with the conviction of Wayne Williams.

Williams was, in fact, convicted of just two of the unholy string of murders of black teenagers and young adults. But the evidence in the lengthy trial involved other deaths in the terrible sequence of murders over a two-year period. Indeed, one main thrust of the prosecution argument was that the evidence in the two murders was convincingly similar to the evidence and pattern in other slayings. The defense had its day and had its say. The twelve jurors who followed the tedious and complex testimony over the long weeks became convinced that Williams was guilty beyond any reasonable doubt.

Atlanta Mayor Andrew Young observed quite properly that Williams has the right of appeal and that there probably will be such an appeal. The mayor also noted that the trial appeared to be fair, that there is no reason to think that the jurors reached anything other than a just verdict.

There is little joy in such a case on any basis, only relief
that a murderer has been captured and tried and convicted,
that he is no longer free to walk about and inflict murderous
harm on others. Yet there are some positive things to be said.

The greater Atlanta community suffered through considerable trauma during the months when some monster in human form appeared to stalk the community, preying on and
murdering black young people. It was a tense and stressful
time. There were some people who behaved badly, who actually
tried to exploit the series of murders for selfish purposes.
There were far more people who behaved well.

There were public officials who worked long, grim hours,
longer probably than their public will ever know, to be sure
that everything possible was being done to stop the killings.
There were Atlanta and Atlanta-area police, state investigators, and FBI agents who worried about every possible theory
and hint of evidence. They weren't getting paid overtime for all
those hours either. It was a national trauma too, not just Atlanta's pain. President Ronald Reagan pledged whatever federal support might conceivably be useful. FBI Director
William Webster aggressively committed his most experienced agents to the case. Indeed, there has never been a case
before, not one, in which FBI agents and local law enforcement
officials worked together so closely.

There were other positive things. A boiler blew up in a day-
care center during a time of great tension about the killings.
Several black youngsters died in the blast. Now, this tragedy
had no apparent connection at all with the string of slayings,
only that the youngsters were also black. But the event
shocked people and increased tensions. Downtown business
folk responded at once; the tragic deaths could not be undone,
but the day-care center could be rebuilt for the living, so the
business community raised hundreds of thousands of dollars
for that purpose.

There was another thing. There was a point in the trauma
when some voices grumbled that there was a racial element in
the investigation, that somehow more time and attention
would be given to the murders if the victims had been white

rather than black. Well, that was never true. The mayor of Atlanta and the public safety commissioner and the police chief were, as it happened, all black. It is a singularly unconvincing argument to suggest that they might care less about the deaths of black young people. Nonetheless, church and community leaders were quick to speak up against that notion, to make it plain in every way possible that the Atlanta community was united in the effort to deal with the fearful random slayings of our children.

There was never any black or white to it, never any rich or poor, not in relation to the general concern of the community. These were our children.

Generations Clash near Mt. Hebron

April 29, 1982

HEBRON, WEST BANK—There was a visible and curious generation gap here, on the road to Mt. Hebron, as Israeli soldiers turned back Peace Now demonstrators. Young Israeli soldiers and young demonstrators, all about the same age, seemed generally friendly and at ease with each other, though on different sides.

The demonstrators wanted to disrupt scheduled ceremonies to establish a new Jewish settlement at Mt. Hebron, here on the West Bank, viewing all such settlements in the Israeli-occupied territories as undercutting efforts at peace. Disrupt? One young woman in the peace group objected to the word. They did not want to disrupt anything, she said, only sing their songs and unfurl their peace signs.

Besides, she said, the army had been unfair. The soldiers had stopped the roughly 100-member Peace Now group for no reason, she said, since they had their signs hidden under their clothes when the army stopped them. A man nearby stared at her curiously. "Don't you think the army knows anything," he asked, adding, "they probably had spies who called them by the time you finished planning this." The young woman was not offended. "I don't doubt it," she smiled.

Oh, it was friendly enough, at least with the young soldiers and young demonstrators, both in their 20s. It got a little hectic, of course, when the situation got out of hand. Dozens of people, not all with the same motivations, pushed past the roadblock in order to walk the mile-plus to Mt. Hebron. The Israeli soldiers, who behaved with grace throughout, were reluctant to stop people by force. Instead, they moved two army vehicles several hundred yards down the road and set up a new kind of roadblock—one of tear gas. It was effective.

But the real anger and passion of the day came from people a generation, even two generations, older than the young soldiers and peace demonstrators. Some were Israeli citizens, some were Americans from a tour bus. They were frustrated because they had wanted to see the dedication of the new Jewish settlement, and that was not working out. The anger came, though, from deeper springs than that.

"Do you know how many Jews were killed here in 1929?" shouted a wiry man. He was white-haired, vigorous, probably in his 60s, and thoroughly outraged. He marched up and down shouting at peace demonstrators. "You are traitors," he yelled, over and over, "You are traitors to the state of Israel."

Hebron in 1929? That was not something I knew anything about. There was an Israeli man standing near me. He had nodded his head in agreement. I asked him, what happened in Hebron? It was a Jewish massacre, he said. The Arabs had wiped out the Jewish community. There were forty or fifty Jews killed, he said, and many injured. The rest fled for their lives.

The young woman who objected to the word "disrupt" was being quizzed by several people about the Peace Now movement. "We are in favor of what we call a sane Zionism," she was saying earnestly.

Americans from a tour bus were the first to make the determined end-run around the first roadblock. They were followed quickly by most of the Peace Now group. The tear gas down the road stopped everybody.

"Uncle, why are they gassing us and not the peace people?" one man asked another plaintively. The tear gas, of course, is indiscriminate, depending on how the wind blows and how close you are.

"Miserable characters," an older man, apparently American, repeated to members of the Peace Now group as they passed. "Miserable characters, the army should push you back hard."

By this time it was really too late to get to the ceremonies at Mt. Hebron. The first car or two started coming back from that direction. The dedication of the new settlement was over. Those who wanted to attend and those who wanted to protest began drifting back toward the first roadblock and their buses and cars.

The dialogue between generations was still going on, however. An older man, whose broad shirt covered an ample stomach, was jabbing his finger at a husky young man with a flat belly, a fellow at least a foot taller. The accent was American. "You're only here because your father and grandfather had the courage to fight," the older one declared, finger jabbing. The younger man said something in a lower voice, not audible from a distance.

"You, you, you," the older man said. "You're chicken."

Part II

Jimmy Carter's Time

Jimmy Carter ran for the State Senate of Georgia in the fall of 1962, just about the time I came to the *Atlanta Constitution* as a reporter.

I met Carter in early 1963, when he came to Atlanta for his first legislative session as a freshman senator, and I was one of several *Atlanta Constitution* reporters assigned to cover the General Assembly. Carter was new and a little hesitant at first, and in our conversations I quickly assumed the role of old battered-but-wise state capitol correspondent, graciously willing to explain to the inexperienced senator from Plains exactly how things really worked. He caught on fairly soon, realizing one day in conversation that this was in fact the first legislative session I had ever covered as a reporter. "You mean you're just as green as I am?" demanded Carter, in mock outrage. I stoutly denied it, of course, pointing out that I had covered some politics for the *Macon Telegraph* and once wrote a political column for the *Yale Daily News*.

Carter was a quick study in the State Senate, competent and intelligent, and he built a certain political constituency there.

One questionable tradition existed of passing a long list of assorted legislation on the very last night of the session. Some few bills were fully understood and properly debated. A great many were relatively minor, perhaps of interest only to a particular legislator or state official, or to some special-interest group—bills that had been carefully held back for a final vote at the last minute. The theory, often accurate, was that a bill that might have trouble passing under normal conditions could sneak through in the confusion of the last night of the session.

It was necessary, of course, that the presiding officer of the Senate, the lieutenant governor, be willing to put such bills on the calendar for the final day of the session. This was usually fine with the lieutenant governor, since this gave him great power in trading political favors. Carter and another senator, Ken Kilpatrick, decided to put a stop to the practice on the last night of the legislative session of 1966. They privately persuaded a majority of their fellow senators that it was a mistake to let these simple "little ole bills," as they were often called, coast through the Senate on the final night, when most senators admittedly had no notion of their impact. Carter and Kilpatrick promised their colleagues that they would research carefully all of these minor bills slated for a vote on the final day, even if this meant staying up all of the night before, and reach a decision on each one. They did just that and on the final night, two dozen plus of their Senate colleagues simply watched to see how Carter and Kilpatrick voted on these little-known pieces of legislation and then voted with them.

Indeed, Carter's friends in the Senate became his only real statewide political base when he began running for governor the first time, in 1966. It was a darkhorse candidacy at best, as his fellow senators understood, yet a half dozen of them campaigned actively in his behalf, contributing substantially with time, money, and other resources.

The essays in this section began in the summer of 1970 when Carter ran for governor the second time, again as an underdog but this time successfully. However, they include comment and analysis relating back to that first 1966 bid for governor. The later columns were written while Carter was governor, then a candidate for president, and later the thirty-ninth president of the United States.

One essay in this section suggests that Jimmy Carter had genuine good luck at critical times in his career, including the climate of the time when he undertook what in other times would have been an exceedingly unlikely bid for the White House. Yet Carter had his share of bad luck too. Any American president probably gets too much credit when things generally seem to be going well, in particular with the economy and global affairs, and conversely suffers too much blame when conditions are troubled. Carter made his mistakes; but he was defeated in 1980 largely because of inflation stemming from the OPEC-nations' hiking of world oil prices and because of our national frustration at the repeated failures to win release for the American hostages in Iran. It is my belief that any president would have had a difficult time gaining reelection in similar circumstances. Carter served this nation honorably as president in many ways, with a distinguished record of great accomplishment. Surely this will be reflected increasingly in the historical accounts of years to come.

Just Ain't
Much Humor
in Politics

July 16, 1970[8]

Judge J. Wilton Carlyle staggered out of the north Georgia hills again the other day, God love him, and confronted me with a baleful stare.

"It's a sorry kind of political summer, son. I'll tell you that," the judge allowed. He peered at me, unsmiling. The judge sat down opposite my desk . . . uninvited, but then judges have certain prerogatives.

"There just ain't any *fun* in it this year," complained the good judge, sadly. He leaned his silver-headed cane carefully against the edge of my desk. That made me happy. When the good judge looks stern, it always make me think he may pick up that heavy silver-tipped cane and break my head. I always

---

[8]The 1970 governor's race was hardfought. Jimmy Carter had run well in 1966, if unsuccessfully, and many of his earlier supporters were determined that 1970 would be his year. Former Gov. Carl Sanders had been barred by the state constitution from seeking a second term in 1966; but he could run again in 1970, and his supporters were just as determined to help Sanders with another term.

speak most respectfully to the judge when he has his cane in hand.

The judge is, I guess, somewhat out of current politics. He used to be a judge, though at what precise level I've never been able exactly to determine. He also served in the legislature once and was a county commissioner for years. His most memorable comment, perhaps reflecting an entire political philosophy, was one simple line: "Friends, given a proper budget and a free hand, I could sell dead cats to the State Board of Health." That was, no doubt, a slight exaggeration.

"Now, it's all very well to raise a little hell and get serious about the *issues*," said the judge, making *issues* sound like a bad word. I smiled, but it was a mistake. The judge immediately frowned and I reared back, thinking he might reach for that silver-headed cane.

"Judge," quoth I, "I don't even want to talk to you about the governor's race."

"Praise God," he said. "I don't want to talk about it either. But, still, you know what I mean. Ole Gene used to get serious and raise hell, but he had some *humor* to it. He could make you mad, but you'd end up chuckling at half the things he said. Marvin's got that gift, too, though my county wasn't for him."

The judge trailed off, muttering a bit to himself. I could make out a few words. "Cufflink Carl . . . Jimmy the Fabricator . . . ," he mumbled ". . . about as much fun as dippin' cows for ticks." He peered at me bleakly, hands on top of his cane. "You enjoying anything about this damnable political summer?" he demanded.

Not much, I allowed, but I suggested that there was one race with signs of good-humored political flair, the battle for the Democratic nomination for a seat on the Public Service Commission between Bobby Pafford and Bob Short.

Pafford, I told the judge, had been bus riding all over the state and handing out copies of Grandma Pafford's Cookbook. He'd also been running classified ads in newspapers, offering to mail anyone interested a copy of said cookbook.

The judge brightened a little, liking the sound of all this. Then, I showed him the classified ad that had appeared in some papers after the Pafford ad had been running for a time. The opposition ad read: "John, Please Come Home. It wasn't my cooking. It was grandmother's cookbook. I've thrown it away. Mary."

This cheered the old judge, and he seemed in better humor when he left. But, as he said, somehow there just ain't much humor in it this year.

Carter Gathers
the Faithful
for Lunch

July 30, 1970

A political luncheon is like a gathering of the faithful.

Former State Sen. Jimmy Carter, candidate for governor in the Democratic primary, announced his formal platform yesterday in the Quality Hotel banquet room in Atlanta, flanked by an American and a Georgia flag. The Carter for Governor banner on the wall behind him has a red-white-and-blue color scheme, *Carter* in blue, *for Governor* in red, all on a white background.

The size of a political crowd is tricky, since candidates sometimes multiply by five and the opposition may divide by 10. But the faithful were out in number for Carter's platform statement. The assistant sales manager at the hotel said they'd set up the luncheon with places for 430 people. The tables were all filled, and there were people standing.

There was a variety of folk. A lot of young people. Some pretty girls with white straw hats and hatbands saying, *Elect Jimmy Carter*, in green letters this time.

There were a good many Atlanta people. Some influential lawyers like Charles Kirbo and Phillip Alston and David Gambrell, and including assorted people from around the state.

The people attending, mostly, were active supporters of Carter in their communities, and they listened intently to their candidate outline his platform.

It's a serious platform with talk of better highways, statewide kindergartens, air and water pollution, more home rule for local communities, and the pledge of a combination of property-tax relief and state grants "equivalent to at least $60 million in additional revenue for our cities and counties."

Carter supporters, the faithful, like the sound of it all. "That is what I wanted him to do," said one man. "He's saying what he's *for*, instead of what he's against."

In the early part of the campaign, Carter attacked his chief opponent in the primary, former Gov. Carl Sanders, as a man who'd abused the governor's power for his personal advantage. A bit later, he hit at the Atlanta newspapers right sharply. Sanders's printed platform ran to just over forty pages. The Carter platform is eighteen pages. When asked if this meant that Sanders was more than twice as interested in the issues, a Carter booster shook his head. "That's probably what you'll say in the paper," he said. Carter himself seemed in good humor, not interested especially in blasting either Sanders or the newspapers.

Maybe one indication of the direction his campaign will take came from the applause his attack on "political expediency" in allotting highway money drew from his supporters. He said later in questions and answers that Highway Director Jim Gillis was supporting Sanders and that if he (Carter) were governor, he would not expect Mr. Gillis to remain in the job.

Making sense out of Georgia politics has never been easy. The conventional political wisdom has Sanders way out front. But the kind of people appearing at the Carter luncheon was impressive. Small predictions: whatever the final outcome, there'll be a Sanders-Carter runoff, and the battle is likely to be hard-fought and close.

Carter No Longer Asks Sanders's Advice

September 14, 1970

It's not likely that Jimmy Carter will be asking Carl Sanders for any political advice in the few days before the runoff in the Democratic primary. But times change, and Georgia politics has always had its share of surprising ironies.

Just over four years ago, at the beginning of the 1966 political summer, State Sen. Jimmy Carter came to Atlanta specifically to ask guidance from Gov. Carl Sanders.

The reason? Carter was of the unhappy view that the Georgia Democratic party was about to go to hell in a basket. He was, at the time, just completing his fourth year in the State Senate and was running for the Third District congressional seat, the seat held by Howard "Bo" Callaway. Yet, by this time, Callaway was in the governor's race, and Carter had already virtually locked up the Democratic nomination for the congressional seat. It looked as though he might be on his way to Washington.

Yet the reason Carter sought advice from Gov. Sanders was that the first unexpected twist of *that* political year had been former Gov. Ernest Vandiver's withdrawal from the governor's race at the last minute because of a heart condition. No one knows what would have happened had Vandiver remained in that race.

At the time most Georgia Democrats (including Carter) believed that Vandiver was the going-away favorite, certain to defeat his two opponents: former Gov. Ellis Arnall and the state's best-known restaurant owner, Lester Maddox.

For a hectic twenty-four hours, it seemed that Sen. Herman Talmadge might come home from Washington to run for governor. Nothing came of that, and a lot of political observers concluded that Ellis Arnall had suddenly become the front-runner and probable Democratic nominee.

Carter, among others, believed Arnall would win the primary. But he feared that Callaway would defeat Arnall in November so overwhelmingly that other Democrats around the state would go down in flames as well (including Democratic congressmen and would-be congressmen).

Carter urged Gov. Sanders and other State Capitol Democrats to encourage someone else to enter the primary, someone who might have a chance to win both the nomination and the November general election.

Carter, apparently, was not yet thinking of himself as a gubernatorial candidate, instead was simply hoping for the strongest possible Democrat at the top of the ticket. Privately, Carter urged both Agriculture Commissioner Phil Campbell and Comptroller Jimmy Bentley to make the race.

It's ironic in retrospect that this year, conceivably, Bentley could have been the Republican nominee for governor and Carter the Democratic nominee. In 1966 Carter offered Bentley his active support if Bentley would run.

Other names were tossed around as possible candidates. One was that of Dr. Noah Langdale, president of Georgia State.

Carter decided, after talking to a good many Georgia Democratic party figures, that no well-known party figure like Bentley or Campbell was willing to run. In early June of 1966 he decided to make the race for governor himself. He's been running ever since.

Sorting Out
Georgia Politics
in the Library

September 24, 1970

Judge J. Wilton Carlyle came limping by the office, late on election day, looking bloodshot of eye and long of tooth, and peering at me in his customary baleful fashion.

"Son, I can't make much out of it," he started out, helping himself to a chair and resting both hands firmly on his silver-headed cane.

"Out of what?" I inquired, suspecting it had to do with elections and campaigns but not sure just where the good judge was headed.

"Never have maintained that Georgia politics made much sense," the judge said, shaking his head, "Never have said that." He peered at me grimly. "You know, more men have been elected between sundown and sunup than ever were elected between sunup and sundown. Now, *that* makes sense. I can understand that. Why, I can remember . . . ," the judge stared out the window almost wistfully, ". . . why, one time my three counties didn't come in with the vote count until three days later." He stared at me again. "Will Rogers," he said abruptly.

Now, it is reported up in north Georgia that in the cool of the day Judge Carlyle will, upon occasion, sip a small libation. It seemed to me, for a moment, that he had perhaps started a bit early, well before the first bullbat could have flown.

"Will Rogers what?" I tried weakly.

"He's the one that said that, about more men elected between sundown and sunup . . . I've been to the library," he said.

"The library," I repeated.

"Yes," he said. "I gave up reading the Atlanta newspapers and trying to understand about the governor's race. You just got me confused. So I went to the library." The judge began fishing around in one coat pocket and his hand emerged with a fistful of slips of paper. "Listen to this," he went on. "*I tell you folks, all politics is applesauce.* That's Will Rogers, too. And this one: *Politics has got so expensive that it takes lots of money to even get beat with.*"

Judge Carlyle sifted through his slips of paper. "Try this one. *Politics ruins the character.* That's Otto von Bismarck."

By this time, I'd entered into the spirit and was flipping through a book of quotations: "Bismarck's also the man who said, *Politics is not a science . . . but an art.*"

The judge nodded. "I thought for a while this one might have something to do with Georgia politics. *What is the first part of politics? Education. The second? Education. And the third? Education.* That's from Jules Michelet. But what did he know? After a while, everybody got tired of hearing about state kindergartens." The judge juggled his handful of quotations. "Now Sidney Hillman understood how some of it worked. He said, *Politics is the science of how who gets what, when and why.*"

"*Politics is still the greatest and the most honorable adventure.* That's Lord Tweedsmuir," I tossed out, flipping pages rapidly. Then, before the judge could comment: "*Get thee glass eyes; And, like a scurvy politician, seem to see the things thou dost not.* Shakespeare."

"Could be son," said the judge, after a moment. "But you can't talk that way on the stump south of Macon."

Jimmy the Greek
Accurately Touted
Jimmy the Carter

November 5, 1970

Jimmy the Greek, a well-known Las Vegas entrepreneur, gave fairly accurate odds on the Georgia governor's race the other day, suggesting that Jimmy Carter was at least a two-to-one favorite.

He also offered a bit of political philosophy with some application to the Georgia results. "Every election looks closer the night before," said the worthy Jimmy the Greek (as distinguished from the worthy Jimmy the Carter).

There was a lot of talk in the closing days of the campaign, especially in the Atlanta area, about the growing support of Hal Suit, the Republican nominee. It's true that Suit got a lot of votes, roughly 400,000. But it's true also that this amounted to roughly forty percent of the total and that Carter's victory margin would run, finally, 170,000 votes or more. In retrospect, on the night before the election, a good many people viewed it as being much closer than it was.

Carter, in a sense, goes into the governor's office with two separate constituencies. He ran for governor the first time in 1966 as a young state senator, generally considered moderate-

to-liberal by those who knew him. Much of his initial support
came from young people, from a handful of state senators, a
few Atlanta attorneys, two or three black leaders who viewed
Carter as a liberal, and some League-of-Women-Voter-type ladies who labored long and hard as volunteers.

The people who worked actively for Carter in 1966 had one
principal thing in common. They tended to be idealistic about
politics. They genuinely wanted a progressive man as governor, simply because he *was* progressive . . . because he was the
best man. Very few of the people working for Carter in 1966
had selfish motivations. The odds were long, and anyone simply looking for a political winner was likely to be helping some
more favored candidate.

Now, this group of people, and it's a sizable group, forms
one Carter constituency. A good many people voting for Carter
this time remembered him favorably from 1966 or thought him
the best man this year, regardless. Nothing in the campaign
changed their minds.

Yet Carter has also a second constituency. The people closest to Carter, those who supported him in 1966 and again this
year, understand that this is true. They tend to get angry
when you mention it (unless it's in the context of saying it's
shrewd political strategy, in which case it pleases them to
mention it).

The suggestion that Carter is a racist incenses Carter loy-
alists. They feel they know him better than that, that it's a be-
low-the-belt sort of insult to suggest such a thing.

There's a good deal of evidence, indeed, to suggest that Carter may be the most liberal Georgia governor on racial matters
ever elected. But he was not elected on that basis. He ran as a
"conservative." In the South, this has meant segregationist.

In 1968 former Alabama Gov. George Corley Wallace carried Georgia overwhelmingly in the presidential election. Wallace's appeal has been that of a racist, an outspoken
segregationist. In his campaign Carter made a strong appeal
for the support of Wallace voters. This doesn't make Carter a
racist, but we live in a time of code words. Hence an appeal for

Wallace supporters is, in some sense, an appeal for segregationist supporters.

Suit, in the closing phase of the campaign, tried to label Carter a "liberal," currently an evil word in Georgia politics. The tactic didn't succeed.

All this isn't to suggest that Carter won as a segregationist. It is to say that many voters viewed him as a conservative, a man who spoke well of George Wallace, certainly not the liberal Suit called him.

Carter has worked hard at preparing himself to be governor for the past four years. He managed, brilliantly, to hold together two disparate constituencies during a long campaign. But it may be that the two constituencies will pull hard in opposing directions as he begins now to put a new administration together.

Counting Heads Among the Carter Forces

February 25, 1971

Judge J. Wilton Carlyle, ever since his own involuntary retirement from the political scene, has become a great watcher
with dubious eye of the various goings-on under the gold dome
of the State Capitol. As he put it once, somebody's *got* to keep
an eye on our assorted lawmakers. If nobody watches, next
thing you know, according to Judge Carlyle, some simple little
old bill will slip through to float a few million dollars in Yazoo
Land Faults Bonds.

"I hadn't figured out yet exactly how the Carter administration works," said the good judge the other day. He'd come to
town on one of his legislature-watching tours and happened
to be here just when the Georgia House was beating down the
proposed two-cents-per-gallon gasoline tax.

The judge sat in my office, put his silver-headed cane carefully on the floor next to his chair, and pulled out a long evil-
appearing cigar. He bit off the end, looked about vaguely, then
finally took aim at a far corner of the room with the same un-
erring accuracy that had given him a certain reputation while
he was a member of the House.

"Now Gov. Carter seems like a nice young fellow. Only candidate I remember who ever came up to the Black Bear Day picnic in my county three years in a row. But he's hard to figure out."

I asked the judge what he meant.

"After a man gets elected governor, he's got a lot of influence. First thing happened with Carter, he tried to get one of his friends elected president pro tem in the Senate. Got beat so bad, I started worrying about his health. It seemed like to me that a man who'd been to Georgia Tech and the Naval Academy ought to be able to at least *count*. Count votes, I mean."

I allowed as how Carter had shown some sign of being able to count better by the time his governmental reorganization plan came to the Senate. The judge nodded vigorously. "That's right. Cracked some heads on that one, but got his bill passed." He sighed. "That's the way a governor used to do it. But, now, this gas-tax bill has got me confused again. Makes me think the governor *still* can't count."

What had puzzled me about it, I told the good judge, was that the Georgia House had passed a gasoline-tax bill for the last two years in a row. Once, it was vetoed by Gov. Maddox, and the other time bogged down in the State Senate. Why all of a sudden did the House change its collective mind?

"How do you think a tax bill gets passed, son?" asked the judge, fixing me with a fierce old eye. "Doesn't just happen. If it's a gas-tax bill, why the money goes for highways, so the highway director is supposed to work on getting it through. That's the system. Mister Jim Gillis was mighty good at it."

I asked the judge how Gov. Carter's choice as new highway director, Calhoun banker Bert Lance, seemed to be doing.

"Oh, he worked at it," said the judge. "They tell me he's been shaking hands, going to bird suppers, urban caucuses, rural caucuses, every-which-way kind of caucus. I saw him after they voted that gas tax down. Felt sorry for him. He looked like a mournful old hound dog. Not sure he knows how to count either."

Catfish,
Turtles,
and Such

December 27, 1971

"Why, hold still, little catfish! All I want to do is gut you."
Judge Carlyle (J. Wilton, that is) is sometimes inclined to
burst into the office, even wax exuberant, but he only rarely
speaks in tongues. I usually have at least a vague idea of what
he's talking about.

"Good to see you, judge," I said, standing up and shaking
hands. He waved me back to my seat and sat opposite me,
hands folded on top of that heavy silver-headed cane.

"Just hold still, little catfish. Won't hurt but a second."
There. He had said it again.

The judge sat there, chuckling. He seemed content. He
might sit there all afternoon. It was clear this was no time to
beat around the bush.

"Just what catfish are we dealing with, judge?" I asked
politely.

"Why, the governor, you ninny!" he roared. "Thought you
liked him, thought you kept up with these high matters of
state politics."

"Hmm," I said, figuring that kept me out of trouble momentarily anyway. The judge rocked back in his chair and started chuckling again.

"So, the governor's a catfish," I allowed. Then, groping a bit desperately: "Last I heard, the governor was a turtle. According, at least, to Secretary of State Ben Fortson."

"Oh, that was good, wasn't it," the judge said. "Said he was as stubborn as a south Georgia turtle, one of those that'll come up to a log and never go around it, just put his head down and push. You know, Ben knows how to turn a phrase . . . ," the judge trailed off, then came back strong, "though I 'spect Ben's had some muleheaded days himself."

It was time to take things in hand. Or try. "Now, judge," I scolded, "here you go carrying on about catfish and turtles and now muleheaded, it's starting to sound like a whole political zoo. You don't even sound respectful."

"Oh, it'll be a zoo all right when the legislature comes to town next month," declared the judge, sounding less respectful by the minute. "They'll all be cruising around on these 14-foot-wide trailers and yelling at each other about the governor's reorganization plan. Hold still, little catfish! Got a whole delegation of high constitutional officers here, just want you to rest easy for a moment, going to talk about an important matter. Won't hardly hurt."

I sighed, "You mean the governor's a catfish because these other elected state officials say they're vetoing part of his state government reorganization plan?"

"Oh, no," the judge shook his head vigorously, "that's all smoke."

"Smoke? But they're supposed to be able to veto anything affecting their departments."

"Certainly," the judge snapped, not accustomed to promiscuous and casual disagreement. "But what does it mean? It just means the legislature votes on those parts of the thing separately. It's not a real veto. Besides, what'd you think they'd do? You give a politician a clear choice between alleged good government and giving up part of his department, and you'll get a veto all right." The judge rolled the word *alleged* around in his mouth with some relish.

"You mean the governor doesn't have any problems?"

The judge looked at me with incredulous eyes. "Not exactly," he said. "You see what the Speaker of the House said about the Health Department? About the fight over reorganizing it and how, just maybe, we ought to study it for a year?" The judge grinned a somewhat wolfish grin. "Hold still, little catfish."

Baptists, Bootleggers, and Whiskey

November 19, 1973

The Baptists and the bootleggers, spiritually speaking, are longtime allies in a number of dry Georgia counties.

It is an unofficial, informal alliance, of course, one sometimes cheerfully acknowledged by the bootleggers, especially at local-referendum election time when they team up (still unofficially, mind you) with Baptists and others to vote the county dry once again. After all, when a county goes wet, it puts the bootleggers out of business.

The Baptists are less eager to recognize this alliance, naturally. It is demoralizing to be fighting the devil and discover that those viewed as the devil's own helpers seem somehow to be on your side.

There is a history behind such curious doin's. The bootlegger's position is perhaps immediately understandable. Vote the county wet and his source of income dries up. But one theory on why the good church people of many dry counties fight the battle so long and hard is that it all goes back to what was called the "Great Experiment." Prohibition supposedly was to end the drinking of alcoholic beverages over the nation. It didn't, of course, and it was eventually repealed mostly because it didn't work, and the profits in illegal whiskey did as much to build up organized crime in this country as probably any other single thing.

Yet in a way the Great Experiment was a great victory in its time for Baptists and other church folk not holding with the evils of drink because it represented a translation of, in their view, moral and religious values into the law of the land. That success meant a lot and, one theory holds, this is one reason why Baptists, among others, continue to fight so fiercely in rearguard actions here and there to prevent liquor sales from becoming legal even in one county and even if illegal whiskey is readily available.

Governor Jimmy Carter is a Baptist himself, but at some point he had the courage to suggest it would probably be better if liquor sales were legal throughout the state.

This amounted to waving a red flag in front of some Georgia Baptists who, at their state convention last week, strongly criticized the governor for such immoral talk, then turned around, incidentally, in a separate resolution to praise the governor for using "his powerful influence for the moral good for all of our state."

Convention President Dr. John Tippett took wry note of the two apparently conflicting resolutions, observing to the convention, "You're an interesting bunch of Baptists."

The governor, when he heard about it, hastily dispatched a letter to be read to the convention, and in it he stated the situation pretty honestly and accurately.

The governor said he had no intention of changing state liquor laws to make dry areas into wet areas, and indeed he added there is little chance that the Georgia General Assembly would pass such legislation.

However, Carter went on, "In every county that professes to be dry, liquor is sold with the full knowledge of community leaders. My point of view is that it is much more serious to condone the illegal sale of liquor in dry counties than it is to sell liquor legally in wet counties.

"The sale of illegal liquor is the nucleus around which additional criminal activities are centered. This criminal activity includes drugs, prostitution, and the sale of pornographic literature.

"The worst part of crime in an organized fashion is in the northeast where most counties are dry. It is important for the Baptists and others to realize that just because a county is dry doesn't mean that liquor isn't being sold."

The governor often talks sense, though in this case probably neither Baptists nor bootleggers like to hear it.

Carter's
Last Year
as Governor

January 21, 1974

It was Friday and the Georgia House had just quit for the weekend, so a fair number of House members wanted a minute or two with the governor before they went home, though his schedule, even for lunch, was running thirty minutes behind.

But, after a while, it slowed up a little and Gov. Jimmy Carter had time to sit down in his office and relax a few minutes over a ham and cheese sandwich and a soft drink and some potato chips.

It is Carter's last legislative session and he knows it. Furthermore, it is the governor's last year of a four-year term and he's aware of that.

Carter may be a lame duck, as the phrase goes, but these days he is relaxed and cheerful and seems confident that as he leaves office most Georgians will view his four-year tenure as one of respectable achievement.

What's on the governor's mind these days? Well, for one thing, he is recovering ruefully from being burned by an old truth that a husband (governor or not) had better be sure he knows what he's talking about when he announces what his wife's opinion is about something.

The governor manfully faced a sizable delegation of women opposing the Equal Rights Amendment for women (ERA) one day last week and told them (not what they wanted to hear) that he was in favor of it. Then, in words that he was to regret, he added: "I might say that my wife disagrees with me on this."

Rosalynn Carter, the first lady, first heard the news that she was one of the anti-ERA crowd that same evening at a bankers' reception for legislators.

"When we got in the car to leave, she spoke strongly to me," said the governor.

It was really just a matter of confusion, said the governor, that he had heard his wife react negatively to some of the more militant women's-lib boosters and that he had teased her about becoming "Ms." instead of "Mrs.," a change she didn't accept. From this he honestly had the impression that she did oppose the ERA. It is not an error the governor will make again.

What about the legislative session? Carter said he is especially interested in no-fault car insurance and a good consumer-protection bill. On the latter, he says, "I'm afraid we could come out with something that was only a re-statement of present law and not really an improvement."

The "biggest and most controversial" bill may well turn out to be the ethics legislation affecting political campaign financing, Carter thinks, and he is convinced that Lt. Gov. Lester Maddox will try to kill or change any such legislation of substance.

It is the last year of four in the governor's chair for Jimmy Carter, and he doesn't seem to have any regrets. "I'd like to complete the last of the aspects of reorganization," he says, this being maybe his top priority in state government during his final year in office.

Carter knows that some parts, specifically the huge Human Resources Department, of his governmental reorganization have drawn fire from the legislators.

"That kind of department isn't efficient in some ways by the nature of it," the governor thinks. "You're talking about health, and welfare, and mental health programs, programs that involve a lot of services for a lot of people." Still, the governor believes the sprawling department will prove itself in the months to come in the most critical way, that of spending less of the funds available on purely administrative activities and more directly on services to people.

Carter finishes his ham and cheese sandwich and potato chips and the rest of his soft drink. Conversation is over. There are other people lined up waiting outside to see the governor of Georgia.

With the Hopefuls
on the Hustings
in New Hampshire

October 8, 1975[9]

MANCHESTER NH—It is fall here, crisp fall. The leaves have turned and feast the eyes with gorgeous hues of red and gold. The seasons change. It will be cold here soon with snow on the ground. Before those snows have melted, the voters of this small New England state may have decisively influenced the 1976 presidential election.

It has happened before. The voters of no other state in the nation exercise such a disproportionate influence on the American political process. In 1960 John F. Kennedy won hugely in this first state primary, a win that started him on the way to winning a string of primaries and took him to the Democratic presidential nomination and to the White House. Last time out, in 1972, Sen. Ed Muskie's supposedly front-running campaign received a crippling blow in New Hamp-

---

[9]Carter's win in the New Hampshire primary gave him critical momentum in his drive for the White House. He became the instant front runner and he remained so in the primaries to come, locking up the Democratic presidential nomination well before the party convention in New York.

shire when Sen. George McGovern made a surprisingly strong
showing. The rigors of campaigning in New Hampshire led
Muskie to shed tears as he stood on the back of a flatbed truck
in front of the newspaper offices in Manchester, an incident
that created more negative comment that it probably deserved,
and yet was credited with helping derail the Muskie campaign
express.

Time passes. It is hard to believe, but the voters will be voic-
ing their presidential preferences in New Hampshire in only a
little over four months. The date of this first state primary has
typically been during the first week in March. Massachusetts
tried to get into the act for 1976 by voting to hold its primary
on the same date; New Hampshire would have none of that and
its legislature promptly moved their date back one week, so
now it will be in February. Just to make sure other upstarts got
the message, the New Hampshire solons also passed a law saying that their state's primary date would be set back again if
necessary, so that it will always be at least one week earlier
than any other state primary.

"This room could well hold the man who is going to be in-
augurated President in January 1977," declared the man at the
podium. It is the Carousel Ballroom in Manchester, and the
man talking is named Larry Radway, a personable college
teacher who ran last year for the Democratic nomination for a
U. S. Senate seat. He lost out but made a lot of friends and later
was persuaded to become Democratic party chairman in New
Hampshire.

There are about 500 people in the room, including six candidates for the 1976 Democratic presidential nomination. The
event is a fund raiser for the state party, $100 per couple, and
first there are cocktails and later there will be dancing until
midnight. In between there are to be speeches. This is a "Presidential Preview," the invitation calls it, with New Hampshire
Democrats playing host to assorted candidates, "and they
want to meet you!" according to the invitation, which accurately adds, "Boy, do they want to meet you!"

The early campaigning is fierce here. The Democrats obviously have no incumbent president, no early frontrunner of

great strength. A potential Democratic nominee can visualize New Hampshire as launching anyone's campaign suddenly into a commanding national position.

Sarge Shriver, brother-in-law of the absent Sen. Ted Kennedy and would-be Camelot heir, is the first speaker. He says a gracious word about one of his Democratic hosts, New Hampshire senior Sen. Tom McIntyre ("Sen. McIntyre would make a great President") and then is off and running for president. He blasts Gerald Ford. "Any Democrat can do better," says he, and then gets into foreign policy. He has just arrived from Moscow, says Shriver, where he had a two-and-one-half hour conversation with Premier Kosygin; and Kosygin told him that the Russians would sign a long-term contract, five or ten or fifteen years, to buy U. S. wheat and also a long-term contract to sell oil to the United States. Not only that, a 1933 treaty permits only one American Catholic priest in Moscow, says Shriver, and he talked about that with Kosygin too. "Asked if that could not be extended, I was told that Soviet officials would look with favor on any request to extend the number of Catholic priests," says Shriver.

One Shriver booster claps loudly at word of this diplomatic triumph, but the Kosygin-Shriver summit otherwise seems to make only a moderate impression on the assembled Democrats. Shriver, though, dresses superbly and has presence; he *looks* as if he might be a serious presidential candidate.

Congressman Mo Udall is next and he jokes, as do other Democrats, about New Hampshire's present, sometimes wild-talking Republican governor. "Your governor wanted nuclear weapons. I want to serve notice that if you get them, then Arizona will conduct a preemptive strike," quoth he. Udall is a good speaker, denounces President Ford for putting up with eight million unemployed, invokes the name of Harry Truman, and says, "You have to go back to Warren Harding to find a President as bad on the environment as Ford." In 1976 Democrats must get together, concludes Udall, saying to the New Hampshire Democrats, "You're going to write the first chapter here in New Hampshire twenty weeks from now."

Sen. Birch Bayh is there too, an all-but-announced candidate, declaring, "Above all, the next President must have the
capacity to make the American people believe again." Bayh
says he wants a president determined to lead America; wants
to break up the big oil companies; wants courage and compassion; and isn't much in favor of the Nixon-Ford "old time Republican economic religion."

Jimmy Carter, former governor of Georgia, takes his turn
and he too wears the dark blue suit and blue shirt that seem
almost required uniform for the assembled presidential candidates. Carter says he has been in forty-three states campaigning since he left the Georgia governor's office, and that
he finds the American people disturbed very deeply about two
basic questions. First, can government be decent, a source of
pride? Second, can the government in Washington be well organized, efficient, and well managed?

Carter's answer to both questions is yes, and he adds that
the people are sick of a government that stands in the way of
progress. He too invokes Harry Truman's name and says that
Truman told his economic advisers early that he wanted policies that meant three things: (1) Jobs for everyone wanting a
job; (2) Low interest rates; and (3) A balanced budget. Those
three goals would be his also while in the White House, says
Carter. He ends his brief speech with another listing of three.
Whatever the nation's problems, he says, there are three
things that don't change: first, that our inherent economic
strength is still there; second, that the strong character of the
American people exists yet; and third, that this nation's system of government is the best on earth.

It is interesting for a Georgian to watch Carter in this New
Hampshire setting. He gets solid applause and seemingly is
taken seriously by the gathered Democrats.

That is not necessarily true of all candidates, such as one
recently announced, Pennsylvania Gov. Milton Shapp, who
comes over as a nice fellow and says the Democrats "need a
candidate not bogged down in Washington, and Jimmy Carter,
I know you will agree with me." Shapp adds that he is a business executive who has been successfully solving problems all

his life. He is a pleasant fellow with the slightly vague look of a man trying to find the Rotary Club meeting in Harrisburg.

Former Oklahoma Sen. Fred Harris is another candidate not taken completely seriously. He is the best speaker of the lot, a stem-winder in denouncing the big oil companies and big corporations ("These industries say they believe in free enterprise. I want to give them a very strong dose of it"), but he too is a little hard to take seriously. One prominent New Hampshire Democrat in conversation referred to Harris as a "spoiler," explaining that Harris was working hard in New Hampshire and would get some votes but that essentially it was hard to believe he had any chance at all for the Democratic presidential nomination.

So, who is doing well in New Hampshire? One New York journalist at the Manchester meeting took a poll of the six or seven bartenders. Carter won, he said, with two votes and the others scattered around. That doubtful poll probably means as much as most predictions. What is interesting, however, is to realize that certain candidates have written New Hampshire off in advance. The New Hampshire Democratic party chairman says that as far as he is aware, Senators Lloyd Bentsen and Henry Jackson and Gov. George Wallace are not making serious efforts in the state. Indeed, he says, at this stage Carter and Bayh and Harris and Udall are the only candidates seemingly working at putting statewide organizations together. Shriver says, when asked, that he has not decided yet about entering New Hampshire.

New Hampshire's primary politics fascinate. There are currently no more than 200,000 registered voters in the entire state. Less than half are Democrats. As few as 35,000 or 40,000 votes might be enough for a candidate to win the 1976 Democratic primary in New Hampshire. People have run and lost in Fulton County Commission races and gotten more votes than that.

And yet on that election night in late February national news media of every description will prepare to send out the results in all directions and read great meaning into those results. New Hampshire is the one state where presidential candidates must campaign almost as if they were running for the local county commission.

Jimmy Carter: The Long-Distance Runner's Progress

October 19, 1975*

Former Georgia Gov. Jimmy Carter is doing probably better in his bid for the Democratic presidential nomination than most citizens of his home state realize. Consider a few random items.

This past week one news story had the figures reported by Carter's presidential campaign committee for the previous quarter. Carter's campaign raised more than $200,000 in the last three months. The campaign is in the black going into the last quarter of 1975, and Carter has already met the requirement for federal matching funds by raising the $5,000 minimum in small contributions in each of twenty states. This means that in January the Carter campaign will qualify for perhaps as much as $700,000 or more in federal campaign money (this, assuming that Carter raises as much money in the fourth quarter of the year as he raised in the last three months).

----

*This essay originally appeared in the Sunday *Atlanta Journal and Constitution*.

Money isn't everything in a political campaign, certainly, but it is important. Carter's campaign has raised more than $500,000 since the beginning of 1975. His campaign organization is spending the money about as rapidly as it arrives. But the money is coming in steadily, if not spectacularly. Indeed, if the financial reports of the various Democratic candidates can be presumed accurate, Carter has already raised more money this year than any other candidate for the Democratic presidential nomination save three: Gov. George Wallace and Senators Henry Jackson and Lloyd Bentsen.

Carter is a distant fourth in that group of Democratic hopefuls in money raising, but that means he has nonetheless done considerably better at it than, say, such worthies as Sen. Birch Bayh or Congressman Morris Udall. Former Gov. Terry Sanford's campaign, incidentally, has already dissolved for complete lack of money; his campaign manager gave up and went back to the practice of law and his staff members have been taking other jobs.

But, money aside, one early indicator of the Democratic primary season has typically been the early caucus states, the states that do not actually hold primaries, but elect delegates to state conventions as early as January, weeks before the first state primary in New Hampshire. Iowa, typically the first such state to elect delegates in such a caucus system, held a straw poll taken at party precinct meetings over the state. The poll showed Carter leading all other Democratic hopefuls. Oh, there was a big undecided vote, and Carter's total was just under ten percent. However, he was trailed by all the other candidates, not bad for a former Georgia governor who was probably totally unknown in Iowa one year ago, until he began campaigning and putting together an organization in that state.

The Associated Press, maybe prodded by that Iowa poll result, did a story last week on Carter's campaign strategy to become a leading contender for the Democratic nomination by scoring well in early caucus states and early primaries. Oklahoma has a caucus shortly after that in Iowa; the AP reports that Gov. David Boren and State Party Chairman Bob Furnston say Bentsen and Carter would be the frontrunners there. New Hampshire? The AP says party leaders have been impressed in New Hampshire with Carter's organization, and the chairman of the state party and the Democratic national committee-woman say Carter will run well in Florida, better than people expect.

Throw into that equation one other factor. Carter intends running in every one of thirty plus state primaries and he is working hard at it. By comparison, we are already seeing the early dropouts among announced candidates. Sanford's campaign is without funds and in shambles. Bentsen has some money and support, but he has recently concluded that he would not or could not run a genuinely national campaign. His campaign manager quit, according to the *New York Times*, because Bentsen refused to make a serious effort in states like Massachusetts and New York. He now says he will run only in selected states, perhaps ten or twelve, and hope to have enough delegates so that he can be a respectable compromise choice at the national convention.

No other candidate in the Democratic sweepstakes is even trying to do what Jimmy Carter is doing, attempting to run all-out in every state primary. It is the effort of the long-distance runner, and the risk is that those continuous eighteen-hour campaign days are of a pace that no candidate can maintain indefinitely. But if those early rumblings from Iowa to Oklahoma and New Hampshire and Florida have meaning, then Carter is making some progress.

How
R. W. Apple
Discovered Iowa

November 8, 1975

Most of the New York- and Washington-based journalists of note are pretty good at what they do, but it fascinates how they continually "discover" this or that, as if it really only became real after they began to write about it.

For instance, somebody in Washington discovered Sen. Hubert Humphrey several weeks ago now, just as if he had been lost in the snow or something, and we have been treated to a whole series of columns and speculative stories about how ole Hubert is really ready to run for president again if the party calls (as if anyone could possibly have had any doubts about that) and how a deadlocked Democratic convention would finally turn to the experienced Minnesota senator as everybody's compromise choice.

It is wonderful, this "discovery" process. R. W. Apple, Jr. of the *New York Times* must have taken the wrong plane or something and, lo and behold, discovered Iowa just the other day, and once out there in that state decided to poll Iowa Democratic leaders. Marvel of marvels, he discovered that Georgia's

Jimmy Carter was way ahead of any other announced Democratic candidate in Iowa.

Now we are in a second stage as people like Tom Wicker, also of the good, gray *Times*, discover Apple discovering Iowa. Where Wicker treads, can Reston or Kraft be far behind?

"Carter?" writes Wicker, in apparent amazement, "Yes, Jimmy Carter of Georgia took a big lead in a poll of Iowa Democratic leaders taken by the *Des Moines Register*. And that may indicate that the press and the politicians—both of whom customarily spend much time preparing to fight the last war—have underestimated the new boys, just as they did in 1968 and 1972."

Theodore White, the maker of many books on the *Making of the President*, has also discovered Carter, at least on a tentative basis.

Last Friday morning Hamilton Jordan and Jody Powell and several other Carter staffers were sitting around a conference table at the Carter campaign headquarters on Peachtree Street and talking about the rest of November and December schedules. Carter doesn't know yet exactly where he will be December twenty-seventh, but this bright, young, hard-working campaign staff will have it figured out to the minute long before December twenty-seventh rolls around.

They are all amused because Teddy White, whose books have become an every-four-years national institution, telephoned, or rather his secretary telephoned, and said that Mr. White had seen somewhere that Gov. Carter was going to be in New York City and he would like to interview him for half an hour or so. She was incredulous when the Carter staff explained that Carter was keeping a tight schedule, with commitments already made, and there wasn't time for Mr. White to spend half an hour or so with the candidate. White himself called later, and it didn't change the schedule any, but the Carter folks said to him that the candidate would be in upper New York State later in November and they would try to work something out for then. No, no, said White, he didn't think he could get out of New York City.

A few Vermont Democrats, speaking of this discovery process, also have discovered Jimmy Carter. An article from the Sunday *Rutland Herald* in Rutland, Vermont, gives an account of a dinner for Carter in Bennington on October 11, one attended by about 400 Democrats, including Vermont Gov. Thomas P. Salmon and U. S. Sen. Patrick J. Leahy. That might have been a matter of courtesy on the part of the elected officials, but one aide to Gov. Salmon, Joseph Jamele, is quoted in the article as saying that Carter is leading all other announced Democratic candidates in Vermont. It is interesting, this process of discovery.

Democrats
Like Carter
in Florida

November 17, 1975

ORLANDO FL—Gerald Rafshoon, looking as cynical as a
defrocked stockbroker, stopped the rather rotund dark-haired
lady in the red dress and asked her suspiciously, "Do you really
think Jimmy Carter could beat George Wallace in the Florida
primary?" The woman chuckled, unintimidated, "Lord, its
about time *somebody* beat Wallace, isn't it?"

The woman moved away, cheerfully, her own mission ac-
complished. She had managed to crowd into the fifth-floor
suite of the Sheraton Towers Hotel to speak for a moment with
former Georgia Gov. Jimmy Carter, presidential candidate and
the clear favorite of the hundreds of Florida Democrats attending their state's first Democratic party convention in seventy-
five years. Those waiting for a chance to speak to Carter filled
the corridors on the fifth floor of the hotel, maybe making a little nervous the Secret Service men who moved unobtrusively
about, keeping an eye on the candidate and on those seeming
so eager to shake his hand.

Rafshoon, Atlanta advertising man and longtime Carter
supporter, watched the woman in red move away. "We're going

to win," muttered he, and while that is the remark of a True Believer, there was considerable evidence at the Florida Democratic meeting that Carter has put together a remarkable political organization in the Sunshine State.

All the Democratic presidential hopefuls were invited to attend the meeting if they wished: the only candidates to show in the flesh were Carter and Pennsylvania Gov. Milton Shapp. The vote yesterday by the Democratic delegates in a straw poll indicating their preference turned into an absolutely incredible showing for Carter as the Plains peanut farmer polled fully sixty-seven percent of the delegates against the rest of the field, 697 votes out of a total 1,035 delegates voting. It is unreal. Carter had more than ten times the vote total of his nearest competitor, Gov. Shapp, whose personal presence at the convention apparently earned him sixty votes. Gov. George Wallace came in third with only fifty-seven votes.

Now, let it be observed at once that Wallace backers do not tend to gather at Democratic party state meetings, whether in Florida or Georgia or anywhere else. Thus Carter's overwhelming margin is not a clear test of any kind of potential Wallace strength. The Alabama governor may well still command the forty-two percent of Florida voters who supported him in the 1972 Florida primary. This is yet to be seen.

But what Carter has done is turn the critical early March Florida primary into a two-man race, Carter against Wallace, and that in itself is remarkable. He has done it by good planning, careful organization, and tireless, effective, personal campaigning (all three adjectives in that last phrase are important).

Other Democratic presidential hopefuls will read the straw-vote result at the Florida Democratic Convention and ponder it and consider whether to make a renewed effort in Florida. Maybe some will try. But at this stage Carter seems to have such a substantial lead among Florida Democrats that a Birch Bayh or a Sargent Shriver has a new worry in considering Florida campaigning. The conventional wisdom is that Wallace will run first in Florida regardless, that the best Carter or anyone might do would be to reduce Wallace's previous vote totals and run a strong second. But can a Shriver or a Bayh risk running well behind both Wallace and Carter? That is the question they now face.

Jimmy Carter
Just Might
Win It All

February 22, 1976*

Jimmy Carter has a chance to break the presidential sweepstakes jockeying wide open, starting with the Tuesday primary in New Hampshire, and he is probably the only candidate in a position potentially to lock up the Democratic nomination early.

This may not happen, needless to say. Campaigns are wild and wondrous things, and there may well be some surprises unanticipated. Yet the consensus among a good many political observers is that of course a lot of things may happen and Carter may not come on as strong in the first primaries as he has done in the first caucus states. But if he does . . . well, as one observer put it, then it's Katie bar the door.

New Hampshire is still the first critical primary state in the nation. It is often full of surprises, such as the time when Henry Cabot Lodge unexpectedly won as a write-in candidate

------

*This essay originally appeared in the Sunday *Atlanta Journal and Constitution*.

while he was ambassador to Saigon. But by anyone's measure Carter is one of the top two or three candidates in New Hampshire. Most say that he and Congressman Morris Udall will fight it out for first place, followed probably by Sen. Birch Bayh and former Sen. Fred Harris (not necessarily in that order).

All right, there is at least a chance that Carter could erupt here, run first and be on the cover of the national news magazines in the following week.

The Massachusetts primary comes exactly one week after New Hampshire. This is an uncertain one; most candidates and their supporters say it is up in the air. Alabama Gov. George Wallace could conceivably, in a split field, carry the only state that went for George McGovern in 1972. And yet Carter has a chance here too. He predicted in Boston and in Lawrence this week that he would at least defeat Wallace in Massachusetts. With a win in New Hampshire just behind him, Carter might run first or second or third, ahead of some of the candidates expected on the face of it to have far more strength in Massachusetts.

So, then that brings us to the Florida primary one week after Massachusetts.

Carter has made Florida virtually a two-candidate race between him and George Wallace. Labor unions and other groups are pledged to Carter at least for the Florida primary in an effort to reduce the potential Wallace strength. Sen. Henry Jackson jumped into the Florida primary quite late, apparently suddenly realizing that Carter might really win and defeat Wallace in a two-man race; yet Jackson's late move leaves him in prospect still only a distant third.

The possibility in Florida is that Carter will at worst run a very strong second, at best could still defeat the Alabama governor even with Jackson in the race. If New Hampshire, Massachusetts, and Florida break in proper fashion for Carter, in a fashion not at all considered inconceivable by political observers in these three states, then James Earl Carter could achieve such tremendous momentum that no one could keep him from winning the 1976 Democratic presidential nomination.

The New Hampshire primary is just two days away; we'll know about that and about Massachusetts and Florida in just two weeks from Tuesday.

Ellis Arnall
Defines
Democrat

March 1, 1976[10]

There was a Great Democrat in that day and time, almost exactly one decade ago, who rose in vigor before his supporters and he declared: "I am a state, local, and national Democrat and anybody who doesn't like it can go to hell."

Many of his supporters clapped and cheered. There were, however, journalists present, and this made some of his most knowledgeable advisers appear grave.

The year was 1966. Only two years before the Republican nominee for president, Sen. Barry Goldwater, had been wiped out in the national election. But he had carried Georgia handily, one of only six states carried by the Arizonan.

The Great Democrat, at that time a candidate for the Democratic nomination for governor in Georgia, was former Gov. Ellis Arnall. His advisers were right to seem grave after his sterling declaration of belief in being a Democrat. That line

---

[10]Ellis Arnall became governor of Georgia at age thirty-five, serving from 1943 to 1947. His administration is generally regarded as one of the most progressive and effective in the state's history.

was one of the things used against him, and it was a time when the national Democratic party was not very popular in Georgia.

Arnall, a progressive and innovative governor in his time, had his share of enemies and many were waiting in the bushes to have at him if he ever ran for office again. They had at him that year in the Democratic primary, many of them to the point of rallying behind Lester Maddox in a runoff in the primary. It was just not the year for a former governor who proudly claimed identification as a state, local, and national Democrat.

Last Saturday night, at the Broward County Democratic Jefferson-Jackson Day Dinner in Hollywood, Florida that same fellow, Ellis Arnall, was speaking on that same favorite subject, what it means to be a Democrat. Arnall quoted a letter from Thomas Jefferson to Henry Lee, a letter dated August 10, 1824, in which Jefferson argued, "Men by their own constitutions are naturally divided into two parties."

One party is made up, wrote Jefferson, of those "who fear and distrust the people, and wish to draw all powers from them into the hands of the higher classes." The other party is made up, he went on, of those "who identify themselves with the people, have confidence in them, cherish and consider them as the most honest and safe, although not always the wisest depository of the public interests."

Jefferson wrote that these two parties have been called by different names in different times: Whigs and Tories, Republicans and Federalists, Aristocrats and Democrats. Today, Jefferson concludes, "we call them Republicans and Democrats."

Ellis Arnall calls them Democrats and Republicans and he makes plain that in his view he and the Democrats are the party identifying with the people, having confidence in them.

"The history of the Democratic party is the story of America's progress and freedom. It is the saga of political strife, political battle, words on paper setting hearts on fire; it is a story of ferment and turmoil; it is the story of every rallying cry for progress and prosperity of the American people. It is the story of the battle for economic freedom, for human rights, for human freedom, for peace in the unceasing struggle for the increasing progress of mankind," said Arnall.

In 1966 Jimmy Carter was one of the candidates running against Arnall. Last Saturday night in Hollywood, Florida, Arnall was introducing Carter to the Broward County Democratic dinner. It fascinates.

Carter's Luck
Is a Factor
in the Campaign

March 20, 1976

There is probably an element of chance, of just plain luck, in any national career, especially a presidential campaign.

Jimmy Carter has had his share of good luck, and it is a part of his enormous campaign success to date. This isn't to suggest that his success is accidental or that he has not earned such success. But watching it all unfold has reminded me, more than once, of a conversation with Bert Lance going back eighteen months ago.

Lance, then, was running for governor of Georgia. Carter was still in office and had not yet formally announced for the White House, but there were already speculative reports that Carter intended such a national campaign. Lance was asked if he believed Carter had any chance at all, since it seemed at the time the most fantastic kind of long shot for a Deep South governor, one just about to leave office, to make a bid for the presidency.

Lance thought about it and said, yes, he thought Carter had a real chance and for two reasons. First, Lance said, Carter would work harder at campaigning and at organizing a national campaign than any other candidate. Second, Carter had good luck; somehow, things just seemed to break for him in a way that nothing else could explain other than that he was lucky.

Somebody else commented at about that stage of Carter's beginning national campaign that the thought of Carter becoming a serious national presidential candidate was like lightning striking, but that whatever happened you could safely predict that Carter would be out there under the storm clouds holding up a lightning rod.

Again, to suggest that Carter is lucky is not to distract from his hard work and effective campaigning. Yet consider the kinds of things that seem to be working for Carter right now, things that no one could really have predicted several years ago when Carter first made the decision to seek the White House in 1976.

Item: There has not been a time in several decades when citizens generally felt so disillusioned about Washington-based politicians. Carter wins applause routinely when he asserts, tongue in cheek, that he has a disadvantage; he is not from Washington. Carter benefits clearly from this anti-Washington sentiment, this sense that the Old Boys in the Congress (and maybe one in the White House, named Gerald Ford) have messed a lot of things up in the last few years and maybe it is a time to look elsewhere for leadership.

Item: No one could have predicted what a weak field of Democratic candidates would seek the White House in 1976. Alabama Gov. George Wallace has less support this year, though he was still considered a dominating figure until Carter defeated him in Florida. Sen. Henry Jackson, Carter's main opponent for the nomination now, could give a fireside chat, as the unkind joke goes, and it would put the fire out. The supposed Liberal Lions of the Left have proved campaign disasters. Only Congressman Morris Udall remains in the field, and he is a weak candidate indeed, making it possible for Carter to expand his moderate-conservative base to the left-of-center wing within the Democratic party.

Item: Carter's very enemies seem to help him. What better recommendation in many parts of the country than to be attacked by Lester Maddox and by George Wallace.

Item: What better issue than to be able in the remaining primaries to run against the "political boys"? The ones who tried, for instance, to keep Carter's name from the ballot in New York State and who increasingly will be trying to find a way to make it a "brokered" convention, one in which the traditional political powers can practice smoked-filled-room politics as usual.

There is a distance of two or three political lifetimes between right now and the Democratic national convention in New York this summer. But so far the Carter luck has stood him in good stead.

Big Wallace Rallies Are No More

March 29, 1976

Done laid around
And played around
This ole town too long
Summer's almost gone
Winter's coming on . . .

That song was hugely popular with the Nashville set a dozen years ago, long before country music took on the same kind of fad appeal that once surrounded Joan Baez on college campuses.

A fellow named Billy Grammer made a hit record of that song and stayed on the charts for a good while. Grammer has been busy these past few months on a special kind of gig, helping warm up the crowds of the faithful at the rallies for Alabama Gov. George Corley Wallace.

Grammer and other country pickers and grinners would come out and flat produce entertainment. Some relatively big names, names that meant something on the "Tonight Show" as well as in Nashville, folk like Bobby Goldsboro, would come on sometimes later as the star attraction. That's how it was down in Miami just the week before the Florida primary, Grammer and the boys and then Goldsboro in the end, and a crowd of a good 5,000 maybe, filling up the south hall of the convention center at Miami Beach. That was the same hall where four years ago in 1972 they rolled out George Wallace in his wheelchair, only weeks after he was shot down in the Maryland shopping center, and he spoke a few words to the national Democratic convention. In pain then he was, bad pain, facing a series of operations to ease infections and repair some of the damage that bullets bounding around in your guts can do.

Wallace told the assembled Democrats in 1972 that the kind of platform they were adopting was going to insure defeat, told some Democratic governors later that he didn't see how he could even support the ticket given the platform, which he couldn't agree with in major ways.

That night in Miami a few weeks ago, Billy Grammer was singing, and Wallace himself was exuberant as the returns from Massachusetts came in. Can you believe George Wallace carried the city of Boston? he would ask in days to come, at other rallies. The Florida primary and Illinois and then North Carolina have come in rapid succession since then.

Billy Grammer was one of the casualties; he was relieved of his duties with the Wallace campaign as were some other musicians and staffers.

The day of the big Wallace rally is over now. Oh, you can reach sometimes 10,000 or 15,000 people at one time, Wallace muses about it, but that really isn't many compared to the total number of voters, and the people who come to the rallies are probably for you anyway. Up in Massachusetts, before the primary there, Wallace's campaign staff tried to buy half-hour segments of time to show entire sections of Wallace rallies. Billy Grammer and the musicians, and the introduction of Alabama's Fightin' Little Judge, and then Wallace himself talking at the crowd almost in punch lines. Welfare, law and order, foreign aid, big government, pointy-headed bureaucrats, busing school children around.

The health issue on Wallace is pretty much of a false one, at least in the sense that the reporters near him and traveling with him find no sign that he wearies easily or is in pain. Yet it tells with many voters. The old, vintage Wallace speech-making ability is there too; he's good at it.

But the times have changed on him, more than Wallace himself; as he points out accurately, other candidates now talk about most of the issues he used to talk about. Has he gone to the well once too often? "I used to have that well pretty much all to myself," Wallace says wryly.

Wallace himself feels it some days, that just maybe he's been layin' around and playin' around this ole town too long.

Changing Candidates
and Confronting
Crazy Minds

April 1, 1976

MADISON WI—Lynn Ansfield is an attractive brunette
with two children, ages 9 and 11, who happens to be on the local school board and who also writes a children's column running in several newspapers.

She also was the Wisconsin coordinator in 1972 for the
campaign of Sen. Henry (Scoop) Jackson. This campaign season she is wearing a green Jimmy Carter campaign button.

Indeed, Ms. Ansfield began the current year as a campaign
coordinator for Jackson, starting out in that role nearly a year
ago. She decided within a couple of months, however, that
Jackson, the candidate for 1976, had changed positions on
some issues since 1972; she withdrew from that campaign.

Several months ago, partly because she reads a number of
newspapers in connection with writing a children's column,
she began to read and follow Jimmy Carter's campaign. She
decided that she liked what Carter said about busing, abortion,
education, and other issues.

Education especially interested her and she valued the notion that Carter had served on a local public school board, as

she does currently. In terms of issues, she especially likes Carter's idea to change the federal revenue-sharing structure so that local agencies of government, cities and counties, will receive this direct federal subsidy while state governments will no longer receive a cut of revenue sharing.

It is not clear whether Ms. Ansfield's shift in loyalties from Jackson to Carter is indicative of any decisive momentum, but it seems possible. Gov. Patrick Lucey says the voting pattern in Wisconsin is "probably still changing" when asked about the outcome of next Tuesday's critical presidential primary here. "You probably have seen the same polls I have. It's a pretty close two-man race," said Lucey. Lucey means the contest for top spot between Carter and Congressman Morris Udall, who has campaigned longer and harder than anyone else in this state, and has said quite candidly that his entire national campaign depends on winning in Wisconsin.

Winner or not, former Jackson state coordinator Lynn Ansfield was at Truax Field in Madison when her former political hero, Scoop Jackson, flew in. She was actually waiting for the arrival of James Earl Carter of Plains, Georgia, as were a number of other Carter boosters. But by coincidence, Jackson and Carter both landed here within ten minutes of each other. Jackson was holding a news conference in a small terminal of this private-plane landing spot at the very moment that Carter's plane was circling the field.

There is meanness abroad in the political land these days, at least here in Madison. It was here a few days ago that several hecklers threw peanuts at Jimmy Carter. That actually is a very mild sort of attack. A heckler spat directly into Sen. Jackson's face at this airfield as he greeted well-wishers after leaving his airplane. Jackson looked tired but seemed unruffled by the nasty incident; local police (not Secret Service) took the young man who inflicted the insult away in handcuffs.

The hecklers at this airport, when Jackson arrived, seemed like the crazies of yesteryears, the yippies and hippies and skippies of several years ago, except their aims seemed even more uninformed. There seemed no issue, no cause involved. A young man whose face literally was painted with broad

black stripes held up a sign as Jackson began his news conference demanding, "America, Change It or Lose It." He was
asked by a reporter if he was protesting any special issue, or
favoring any special candidate, and his answer was, "None of
the above."

The crazy minds in Madison, Wisconsin, are probably in a
small minority. Neither Jackson, nor Carter, nor other candidates typically experience even mild peanut-throwing sorts of
incidents. But there is a terrible cruelness of spirit in what
happened to Alabama Gov. George Corley Wallace in this city
one day this week as he spoke to a civic club; his several hecklers came in wheelchairs and each wheelchair pusher wore a
face mask with an Arthur Bremer likeness—likeness, that is,
of a man convicted of shooting Wallace down in the Maryland
shopping center in 1972. That is genuinely ill of mind.

On the Making
of a Political
Phenomenon

April 29, 1976

PHILADELPHIA—The shrill, ear-shattering Rebel Yell made it sound at the least as if the Yankees were coming again, and it attracted an immediate crowd to the dapper white-haired man in the ballroom of the Sheraton Hotel here. He was standing in front of one of the several television sets around the room, and he yelled a couple more times for good measure as people crowded towards him.

It was only minutes after the polls closed in Pennsylvania, and the results were coming in earlier than expected with the first signs of Jimmy Carter's stunning victory in this large industrial state.

The Rebel Yeller, one Lewis Flynn of Thomasville, grinned almost as widely as his candidate tends to do as the first returns were reported on the television screen. He has something else in common with Carter, being a peanut farmer, though he has several other farming and business interests as well. Flynn and wife Diana are among the Georgians who invaded Pennsylvania the week before to campaign actively for James Earl Carter of Plains. Mrs. Flynn reports that it was an incredible week, one they would not have missed. The results on election night make it all seem more exciting than ever.

Jimmy Carter's national campaign for the White House is without question the most remarkable political phenomenon in the nation since Wendell Wilkie emerged from nowhere more than thirty years ago to capture the Republican presidential nomination. The nearest comparisons to the Carter campaign go back, perhaps not to Wilkie, but to the campaigns of 1956 and 1960 on the Democratic side.

In 1956 Sen. Estes Kefauver rode out of Tennessee wearing his coonskin hat and began furiously shaking hands and courting votes in primary states. Kefauver was a remarkable person-to-person campaigner. Carter himself is genuinely flattered when some older Democrats occasionally remark that Carter works as hard at campaigning as did Sen. Kefauver. But Kefauver was relatively weak on planning and organization beyond that great skill at face-to-face campaigning. He probably never really had a chance at the presidential nomination of his party, though he did receive second place on the Democratic ticket with Adlai Stevenson in 1956.

Carter's campaign has, however, more in common in many ways with the John F. Kennedy campaign of 1960. Kennedy was a good campaigner certainly, but he was also a planner and an organizer. Carter has considerable skill, as did Kennedy, in attracting and using bright and competent staff people and volunteer workers. No candidate in memory has succeeded, neither Kennedy nor Kefauver, in persuading literally hundreds of citizens from his home state (like the Flynns) to spend their own money and days and weeks of their time to go to states halfway across the country to knock on doors and campaign actively.

Carter and his closest advisers believe that Pennsylvania, as Carter put it, "wiped out" his active opposition for the Democratic presidential nomination. There clearly exists still some ABC (Anybody But Carter) sentiment within Democratic ranks and Sen. Hubert Humphrey still waits in the wings in hopes that the Carter momentum will falter, giving him a chance to become the presidential nominee. But there seems less and less chance of such compromise moves after Carter's stunning win in Pennsylvania and the very likely possibility that he will do well in Texas and Louisiana primaries this Saturday and in Georgia and Alabama and Indiana primaries next Tuesday.

Of course, Carter could blunder in some fashion, and that would change the odds. But as a number of national media types have observed, the most significant thing about the "ethnic purity" controversy may really be that Carter indeed put his foot in his mouth, yet then recovered, remaining very cool under considerable pressure and coming through the controversy without suffering any mortal political damage. It is this kind of race under pressure that is appreciated by the Democratic party political pros who have doubts about Carter, in part simply because they felt they did not really know him.

Theodore White wrote in his first "Making of a President" book about the 1960 campaign that a national presidential bid often emerges from a state political party that happens to be full of energy and vitality and competence. That is true in a real sense of the Carter campaign. Carter personally has enormous energy and stamina and drive. He worked hard at being governor while holding that office in Georgia, yet seemingly found time to begin planning all the details of a national political campaign. His chief staffers in that effort worked for him in his successful governor's campaign, some going as far back even as his first run for the governorship in 1966.

Hamilton Jordan, now national campaign director, was Carter's executive secretary, then went off to Washington to work for a year or so for the national Democratic committee, part of a conscious effort to begin getting ready for Carter's national campaign. Jody Powell, Carter's press secretary at the state capitol, now handles the national press with considerable good humor and skill amid the routine confusions of the campaign trial. To call Gerald Rafshoon the campaign ad man is a bit like calling a Stradivarius a fiddle; Rafshoon goes back to the 1966 Carter campaign, and he is as much adviser and friend as ad man, though his political advertising for the Carter campaign gets high marks.

These are some of the familiar faces of the Carter campaign, going back to Carter's statewide political races, and they were all on hand at the Carter headquarters at the Sheraton Hotel Tuesday night.

Georgia State Rep. Ben Brown was on hand, one of the key black supporters who has meant so much to the Jimmy Carter campaign. It is one of the remarkable sides to this campaign that a white Southerner has received his most consistent and significant early voting support from black voters over the nation, a tribute to the effort of Rep. Brown and Atlanta Congressman Andrew Young and Rev. Martin Luther King, Sr., and a host of others. Atlanta Mayor Maynard Jackson's recent endorsement of Carter will undoubtedly help add to this basic and key segment of what might be called the Carter coalition.

But there were the new faces too, and a major reason for Carter's success has been this ability to attract good people.

Pat Caddell was there, the young professional pollster out of Harvard who did an incredible job for George McGovern in 1972 and who this year has gradually (after swearing privately he would never become so involved with a candidate again) developed into a Carter booster of the highest order. Tim Kraft was around, the gifted one who put together the Carter organization in Iowa, where Carter's surprising strength in the first caucus state initially caught national attention. And there was Phil Wise, the son of an old, close friend of Carter from Sumter County, who coordinated the Florida organization, which put together Carter's win over Alabama Governor George Wallace.

There were also some relatively new faces on hand, people who are already playing significant roles in the national campaign.

Dick Weinstein, a Connecticut attorney who is now director nationally of Citizens for Carter, was on the scene. Weinstein, like Caddell, has found himself gradually pulled more and more into the campaign. He says he was on a kind of "sabbatical" from his law firm in Florida when he got involved in helping Carter, first only in Florida, and now over the country. Another clear asset for the Carter national effort is another attorney, William J. vanden Heuvel. Vanden Heuvel is a New York attorney, was a friend and admirer of the late Sen. Robert Kennedy and was active in Kennedy's 1968 campaign until it ended with the tragic assassination in California. He worked to help Carter in the New York primary and has now undertaken functioning as "issues" adviser, probably expecting to travel with Carter a fair amount of the time. He is good and has already done his homework. A news magazine reporter asked Vanden Heuvel on the press bus, what had Carter's position on Vietnam been several years ago? Vanden Heuvel was able immediately to quote a Carter statement from February 1971, made only a month after Carter had taken office as governor. Carter was pressed for details on an economic question at a reception-fundraiser in New Canaan, Connecticut, late one evening; Vanden Heuvel was on the telephone early the next morning seeking further details, which Carter might use in future answers.

If Carter's national campaign continues its successful momentum, he will need such additional help.

What is already incredible, however, is that a Southerner, a former Georgia governor, has already emerged in this 1976 election year as the going-away frontrunner for the Democratic presidential nomination. He may yet become, as Carter himself told an audience jokingly one evening (though he certainly meant it too), the first farmer to sit in the White House since Thomas Jefferson.

Firing
Henry Grady's
Cannon

October 31, 1976[*][11]

The brass cannon, mounted on steel wheels and with a red base, was cast at the request of then *Atlanta Constitution* editor Henry Grady back in the early 1880s.

Grady, spokesman of that earlier New South, believed it likely that the Democratic party would reclaim the White House for the first time since the Civil War in 1884. He asked a friend in the foundry business to cast the small but solid little cannon as an appropriate method of celebrating the na-

---

*This essay originally appeared in the Sunday *Atlanta Journal and Constitution*.

[11]My time estimate was a little optimistic. It was about 1:00 A.M. when the late returns from Mississippi assured Carter of enough electoral votes to become our thirty-ninth president. Publisher Jack Tarver and I fired the cannon (with ears ringing) in front of Henry Grady's statue at the intersection of Marietta and Forsyth streets. Then Associate Editor Bill Shipp and I, stoutly aided by editorial board members Lee May and Gene Tharpe, moved the cannon near the Omni (where the president-elect and supporters were celebrating) and fired it many more times. The Secret Service did not entirely approve.

tional election of 1884, should indeed Grover Cleveland succeed in ousting the Republicans from the presidency.

It was a close election that year of 1884, and the returns were not clear until the next day. Then, when it was over and Cleveland had won, Grady and friends fired that brass cannon in celebration.

Editor Grady may have had a prophetic sense of his own short life. For the Republicans won the White House again in 1888, and thus in potential the Democrats might have had a chance to reclaim the White House once again in 1892; Grady loaded the cannon himself and pasted a slip of paper over the touch hole and then stored it with a letter saying that he hoped to live until 1892 and once again celebrate the victory of a Democratic president. But he added in a postscript to the letter that if he should not be among the living, he hoped his friends would fire the brass cannon in front of the *Constitution* building and let the blast alert Atlantans that the Democratic nominee had won yet again.

Alas, Grady died of pneumonia on December 23, 1889. But his friends remembered and on election outcome in 1892, when Cleveland won again and regained the White House for the Democrats, the cannon was brought from storage, still with Grady's charge intact, and the fuse was lighted and the election outcome celebrated with a thunderous sound.

That same brass cannon sounded again in 1932 when Franklin D. Roosevelt was elected, and then it was retired to the inactive ranks until 1960, fully twenty-eight years later.

In 1960 the late Ralph McGill and friends hauled the cannon forth once more in considerable exuberance and fired it in front of Henry Grady's towering statue in downtown Atlanta, looking south towards Five Points from Forsyth and Marietta streets. McGill, an old Marine, was alleged to know more about cannon firing than some of his dubious cohorts. He fired off the fuse in grand style and produced a resounding boom and blast. He also managed to let the cannon recoil severely against one leg and to singe his eyebrows, and the three police cruisers who raced to the scene of the blast found McGill hobbling about, cheerful of spirit but limping some, too.

This now-famous (or notorious) brass cannon is fired formally only when a Democratic presidential nominee reclaims the White House and wins the presidency, like say this Tuesday night when the votes are counted.

It'll be time to fire Grady's cannon, I would estimate, somewhere around midnight.

Those Early
Risers Lean
to Mischief

December 10, 1976

George Busbee and Jimmy Carter are both inclined to get up early in the morning, which gives them extra time to get into mischief on some days, and they were both up to some mischief one morning this week.

Governor Busbee was entertaining his immediate predecessor in that office, now President-elect Carter, and the two men were up in the governor's second-floor office at the mansion a few minutes before 7 A.M., drinking coffee and talking about one thing and another.

Busbee told Carter that former State Sen. Bobby Rowan, the pride of Enigma, wanted to be on the state Board of Human Resources and Busbee had been trying to work it out but it was a little difficult; the law requires a certain number of physicians to be on that board, and so Busbee had been juggling around with upcoming vacancies and he told Carter that he had finally worked it all out and planned to let Rowan know.

This was when the mischief started. Carter served with Rowan for four years in the State Senate and worked with him later while governor. Busbee too knew Rowan in the legislature, and the two were friendly opponents in the 1974 governor's race. Rowan, a forty-one-year-old farmer-businessman in Enigma, is a colorful, outspoken fellow, one of the best political storytellers around, almost impossible not to like if you stay around him for five minutes, and both Carter and Busbee indeed do like him.

The two schemers on the second floor of the governor's mansion got a state patrolman to call Rowan down in Enigma, this before 7 A.M., and the call apparently woke him up. The patrolman had been coached to say, "The Governor is calling," but without saying which governor, and Rowan clearly expected to hear Gov. Busbee's voice come on the line. Instead, former Gov. Carter started in talking to Rowan, wanted to know how he was and how busy he was, and could he possibly come up to Atlanta that afternoon? Rowan allowed as how it was a busy time in Enigma but maybe he could make it.

Well, said Carter, I think I can talk Gov. Busbee into naming you to the Board of Human Resources, would you accept it if he'll name you?

Rowan said, yes, he thought he would like that, and Carter handed the telephone to Gov. Busbee. "Bobby, he just talked me into it," Busbee said.

Rowan reportedly said something quite rude to the present governor of Georgia, but you will not read such talk here. Then, Rowan went on: "George, I thought I was about to be at least ambassador to Angola."

Angola's loss, of course, is the Human Resources Department's gain. Rowan will give that board some additional strength, both as one who cares deeply about the people and programs involved and also as one with excellent ties to Gov. Busbee and to members of the Georgia General Assembly.

High Public Official Waits in the Cold

December 20, 1976[*]

Washington notes: This tall, big fellow stood pacing about on the sidewalk in front of the government building, not far down from the White House, and complained good-humoredly that it was cold and he did not have an overcoat and where was Jack Nelson anyway?

"Nelson," asserted the man sternly, when Nelson appeared, "you have been keeping a High Governmental Official waiting out here in the cold. That's a terrible thing." The man glanced at his watch. "You have kept a High Official waiting for fourteen minutes, standing around in twenty-three degree weather," he declared.

He and Nelson then walked three or four blocks through the cold to the High Official's hotel where Nelson, Washington bureau chief for the *Los Angeles Times*, wanted to interview him. The weather was cold enough, actually probably closer to

---

[*]This essay originally appeared in the Sunday *Atlanta Journal and Constitution*.

thirty-three degrees than twenty-three, but it got colder as the High Official told the story again a little later, to someone else in Nelson's presence. "He kept me, a High Government Official, waiting in the cold weather for fourteen minutes in twenty-three degree weather, or maybe it was for twenty-three minutes in fourteen-degree weather. It was one or the other," said High Official.

The High Official standing in the cold was Atlanta banker Bert Lance, in Washington to make plans for his new assignment as President-elect Carter's choice to be director of the federal budget, head of the Office of Management and Budget (OMB). He finds a good deal of the High Official ballyhoo of official Washington fairly funny and jokes about it. One day another journalist, a Chicago reporter, wanted to interview him and Lance was keeping a tight schedule, but told the reporter that he could go along with him to his next appointment if he wished and talk on the way. The reporter said fine, then reacted in amazement when he realized Lance meant to actually walk to his next appointment (five or six blocks away). Don't you have an official car? the reporter wanted to know.

Lance spoke to the Washington Press Club earlier this month and told the audience that he had already discovered that people in Washington looked at you doubtfully if you did not know them and just said hello. "You try to shake hands, and they may call the police," said Lance. Lance himself, not a typical thing for a Cabinet-level official, spent a few minutes at the Washington Press Club moving around the room and shaking hands with everyone and suffered a minor setback. There was one man playing backgammon while he ate lunch, very intently, and Lance spoke to him, determined to shake hands with the man. Lance extended his hand, and the backgammon player stabbed it (accidentally) with his fork. Ah, such are the setbacks for new High Public Officials.

There was one part of the official Mickey Mouse that Lance found less amusing. He tried to drop by OMB, the agency he will head in the Carter administration, and eventually got in the door, but only after the security guards had taken his photograph, fingerprinted him, and demanded several pieces of identification—no doubt trying to be doubly sure that this particular 6-foot-5 Bert Lance with a Southern drawl was the right one. They made an impression on the new OMB director all right, but it might not have been exactly the impression they intended.

Carter
and Editors
and Telephones

May 10, 1977

HONOLULU—Tom Winship of the *Boston Globe* deserved it without any doubt, to be rung in as an addition to the panel, bright red sports coat and all, and to be in that more or less foolish position of being stuck there in the flesh and trying to talk to the distant, disembodied voice on the telephone, even if that voice did happen to be that of the president of the United States.

President Carter was in the White House, about 4:45 P.M. that afternoon, and his telephone call was being received in Hawaii some thousands of miles away at 10:45 A.M. If that sounds confusing, it's because that is the way newspaper editors in a group do things: confusingly.

Winship fully deserved to be there on that panel for his sins. One year ago the American Society of Newspaper Editors met (as the ASNE usually does) in Washington, and Winship was presiding over another telephone session. It wasn't intended as a telephone encounter. The presidential candidates still fighting it out for the Democratic nomination were supposed to be there in the flesh—Sen. Henry Jackson and Congressman Mo Udall and that ex-governor of Georgia (what's his name?), Jimmy Carter.

Anyway, some striking television technicians put up a picket line that morning (actually a picket line that was gone before the candidates were supposed to appear), and the candidates all decided to be somewhere else, except that they did all talk to the assembled editors over a telephone hookup.

Telephone hookups are notoriously unsatisfactory. There is something about just not seeing a speaker that makes such sessions seem as thin as smoke. As somebody wrote about that Washington session last year, Sen. Hubert Humphrey showed up to speak at the luncheon and he could have said "Bow, Wow, Woof, Woof," and been ringingly applauded, just because he was actually there, in the flesh.

Winship did the best he could the other day, by this time no doubt having become accustomed to presiding over disasters. He and Joe Parham, editor of the *Macon News*, and Dave Broder of the *Washington Post*, and a Japanese journalist, Yukio Matsuyama, whose paper has seven million circulation, all asked questions of President Carter by long-distance, and then afterward talked about Carter's first 100 days.

Parham may have had the best line. Carter had made some friends and enemies in his first 100 days, said Parham, and he would list some of Carter's enemies in no particular order as Doonesbury, Idi Amin, Lester Maddox, and David Broder. Broder looked mildly dismayed to be put in such company.

Carter has not had much luck with speaking to the ASNE. The annual session was held in Atlanta several years ago while Carter was governor of Georgia; the nearest he came to being on a program was when his first cousin, Don Carter, took him to a luncheon or whatever and got him introduced. Last year and this year, he was on the telephone to ASNE, a hard way to do it. Two years ago several candidates for president were invited to speak, Carter not among them, not considered at the time a "major" candidate by the wise old editors.

Next year? The editors are back in Washington again, and President Carter hinted that he just might appear in the flesh. He even had a friendly needling word for the *Boston Globe* and

Tom Winship. He had meetings with the *Boston Globe* earlier, Carter noted, and he hoped that the next "is more productive politically."

On Rights
(for Rich
Women Only)

*July 17, 1977**

President Jimmy Carter is simply wrongheaded, in my opinion, in his stand against using federal money for abortions, except in the most extreme cases involving the life of the mother or rape or incest.

Recent court decisions have held that the federal government is not required to finance an abortion, and Carter noted that these decisions were compatible with his own personal belief on the matter.

Asked at a news conference, he did not try to dodge the critical question, namely that the court decisions and his own policy on the matter in practice mean that a wealthy or even moderately well-to-do woman has the choice of a safe, convenient abortion, while a poor woman no longer has that choice, unless you count the kitchen-table butchers who so often have performed abortions on the poor.

---

*This essay originally appeared in the Sunday *Atlanta Journal and Constitution*.

There are "many things in life that are not fair," said Carter, "that wealthy people can afford and poor people can't. But I don't believe that the federal government should take action to try to make these opportunities exactly equal, particularly when there is a moral factor involved."

Well, Carter makes an interesting case with that comment. It has something of the ring of the late President John Kennedy, who once observed in a different context that life itself is unfair. That is true enough, but it seems to me we are talking about something different here.

Of course, life is unfair, and of course there is a moral factor involved in any question of abortion. And Carter was quite right when he observed more than once in the presidential campaign that abortion is one of those complex issues with deep moral, religious, and ethical implications, an issue that will not be solved in this generation. That is, people a generation from now are likely to be still debating the various moral sides of the issue, no matter what court decisions or public policies are arrived at in this year of 1977.

But I think what troubles me most about Carter's position is that the moral factor involved in abortion is such a personal one, and that a federal policy refusing to let the moral choice be an individual choice in fact forces a choice on any number of individuals. There is plainly something wrong in saying, all right, this is a moral question, but you have to have money enough to be able to afford even considering the question. Back to the starting point, to say that federal funds cannot be used for an abortion (except in extreme cases) is to say that a middle-class or wealthy woman deserves the luxury of moral choice and a poor woman does not.

The Supreme Court, even in its recent decision that the federal government does not necessarily have to provide funds for abortions, confirmed again its basic ruling that indeed an individual woman with the advice of her doctor has the right to decide to have an abortion.

There is something terribly unjust in denying a constitutional right to any woman simply because she is poor.

Playboy,
the President
and the Bishop

August 3, 1979

Jimmy Carter has been stealing Griffin Bell's lines again. Former Attorney General Bell was in the audience out at Emory Thursday, a witness to the crime, as President Carter spoke to those assembled for the groundbreaking of a $3.5 million new chapel building.

It is one of Bell's favorite stories, a story about one of the more famous Protestant ministers, John Wesley. Wesley never cared much about earthly possessions, as Bell tells it, and when Wesley died someone asked about his estate. What had he left behind? Just four silver teaspoons, that was all. Four spoons . . . and the Methodist Church.

Bell used to tell that story to people whom he was trying to recruit into the government, trying to make them see that whatever sacrifices public service might mean, there were the possibilities of significant achievement, of leaving a legacy. It hooked a few, that story.

Carter told that story at the beginning of his Emory address and made it something of a theme. Neither an individual nor a nation can be measured in any of the objective, materialistic ways, he said—only in the end by the intangible things, the sense of values and beliefs that go beyond the materialistic. His theme took up again that speech he made meeting with so many different Americans on Camp David, the concern that the country faces something of a moral crisis, and the need to apply the best of our own personal values to the most complex kinds of problems in the present world. The problems are terribly complex and difficult, Carter argued, but quoted historian Arnold Toynbee as saying such difficult times had as a rule been also the times that produced great achievement. Nations had declined more obviously during times of complacency, said Carter.

Perhaps the most significant specific remarks in Carter's Emory address turned to the current controversies involving United Nations Ambassador Andrew Young, not just Young's resignation but the visible signs of deep bitterness in some cases between black and Jewish Americans over the issues that led to the resignation.

Young had been scheduled indeed to offer the invocation at the groundbreaking ceremonies, but was called back to New York for an American emergency meeting of the U. N. Security Council. Carter observed that he very much regretted that Young was not there too and went on to praise the U. N. ambassador in glowing terms, saying that Young had helped literally millions of people in the developing countries of the world understand that the United States wanted to be on their side in the best sense of supporting justice and individual aspirations in every part of the globe.

Carter invoked issues in the aftermath of Young's resignation, such as the expressions of violent feelings between black and Jewish Americans. Such a split should not be permitted to occur, said Carter, because both groups of Americans had known persecutions and had fought hard for equal opportunities and because both were too important to America as a whole.

Carter had a lot of friends at the Emory luncheon and the groundbreaking ceremonies, and the tone was often good-humored. D. W. Brooks remembered how he would have lunch with then-Gov. Carter and usually be lucky if he got one sandwich. One speaker offered a rabbit reference, conjuring up the story of that alleged Killer Rabbit that tried to attack the leader of the Western world while he was fishing. Methodist Bishop William R. Cannon, the man in whose honor the new Emory building will be named, remembered something Carter once did for him. It was just after the controversial Carter interview in *Playboy* magazine, and the bishop was at an airport and asked a younger associate to go buy a copy of *Playboy* and slip it secretly into the bishop's briefcase.

The secret mission went well until the bishop went through security; the machine broke down that X-rayed luggage and the bishop had to open up the briefcase, with *Playboy* magazine prominently displayed on top. That's when he discovered again, Cannon noted, that your sins will find you out.

Griffin Bell
Served This
Nation Well

August 20, 1979

WASHINGTON—The broad, open courtyard at the Justice Department was crowded with people last Wednesday evening, falling roughly into what some called the Georgia Crowd and the Baltimore Crowd.

The Georgians were there to celebrate Griffin Bell, the outgoing attorney general of the United States, who good-humoredly made the rounds, making little secret of his delight at the prospect of heading home to Atlanta and the practice of law. The Baltimore folk were there in honor of Benjamin Civiletti, their native son, Bell's deputy and now slated to be sworn in as the new attorney general.

The courtyard was an appropriate place for such a hail-and-farewell gathering. Robert Kennedy's last official act as attorney general was within this courtyard, speaking to some 2,000 Justice employees in a farewell before he left to run for the U. S. Senate. There was music that day, a group playing "When Irish Eyes Are Smiling." Four years later Kennedy was dead, shot down by a fanatic in a California hotel on the night of the California presidential primary.

There is a metal sculpture, a bust, of Robert Kennedy in the courtyard today. It rests on a small stand at the edge of the raised center section, near the fountain and the flowers and greenery. It catches something of the spirit of Bobby Kennedy even as the bust by the same sculptor, Robert Berks, catches something of the spirit of the late president, John Kennedy. That one is in the Kennedy Center.

Griffin Bell was mildly appalled at the state of this courtyard when he first came to the Justice Department. The flowers and greenery had been let go. The walls of the building around the courtyard looked as if they had not been cleaned in a while. One of Bell's first minor actions in Washington was to light a fire under the GSA maintenance people to put that courtyard right. In far more major ways, he moved decisively to put some other things right over the next two years and seven months.

> When Judge Bell first came to this Hall
> His detractors predicted a fall
> But they all stayed to cheer
> As the parting draws near
> And we're sure going to miss his y'all.

That limerick was written by Solicitor General Wade Mc-Cree, a distinguished fellow whose merits should not be judged by the quality of his verse (limericks, after all, are a temptation of the devil). McCree indeed is a visible sign of one of Bell's strong suits, the ability to recruit distinguished people for top government jobs. Bell knew McCree when both were federal judges and the solicitor general (along with other Bell appointees) has received high marks for performance in his job.

The people attending the reception the other evening in some ways seemed almost to represent the areas of concern facing the Justice Department when Bell came to Washington.

There were Congressman Peter Rodino, who presided over the Watergate hearings in the House, and Judge John Sirica, who actually handled the case of the Watergate break-in in federal court. Sirica once asked Bell's advice on whether he should write a book about Watergate, and Bell suggested that Sirica first resign as a judge but write the book by all means. It was important history. One of Bell's major achievements has been to restore the prestige and nonpolitical reputation of a Justice Department badly tainted by the Watergate scandals.

William Webster, the new FBI director, was there, too. Webster is another federal judge lured by Bell from the security of a lifelong judicial post to take on a tough job in the wilds of Washington. Webster has already moved a long way to restore morale within the FBI and to the agency's reputation in general.

Other significant areas that concerned Bell included guidelines for American intelligence agencies, white-collar crime, and presiding over the selection of more new federal judges than have ever before been named at one time.

Bell was blasted as a country-club racist at confirmation hearings, but he became the first attorney general with the courage to put a black attorney, a highly qualified one, in charge of the Justice Department's Civil Rights Division.

Bell's closing days in Washington were marked by quite remarkable tributes from those who were his most outspoken critics at the time President Carter tapped him to be attorney general. Other Georgians, Carter included, are not faring so well. "Are you from the same country we are?" Hamilton Jordan, White House chief of staff, asked Bell one day.

Bell, always candid, told reporters at a breakfast a few days ago that the president ought to fire some of the amateurs in his administration. Carter had made a mistake, he added, in appearing to be so anti-Washington-establishment; you almost have to become part of that establishment to get anything done, in Bell's view. That outspokenness does not seem, however, to undercut Bell's close ties to the president. Carter sent Bell a handwritten note within hours of the time news stories appeared with those Bell quotes. It was tongue-in-cheek, saying, "Thanks! I'll come over tomorrow and do the same for you," referring to the scheduled ceremonies for Bell's departure and the swearing-in of the new attorney general. The note was signed "Jimmy, Neo Establishmentarian."

Wade McCree yielded to the devil and composed one other farewell limerick:

There are few who can rival his style
And he turns away wrath with his smile
This Georgia High Stepper
Enjoys Rooster Pepper
And he brightened our lives for a while.

That reference to Rooster Pepper spicy sausage may have a curious ring for future historians. The considerable achievements of Griffin Bell as attorney general of the United States will be easier to define. Bell has served his nation well. Georgians have special reason to be proud of him. Nice to have him home.

It Took
Courage
to Try

April 26, 1980*

President Carter appeared incredibly vulnerable, as one of my colleagues put it, when he appeared on television early Friday morning to announce the death of eight Americans in an aborted effort to rescue the American hostages in Iran.

Carter had already been up all night. His sorrow at the loss of those lives, his regret that the effort to save the hostages had come to naught, were plain. He took full responsibility for the decision to try and for the failure. That is proper; he is, after all, the commander in chief.

He is also a commander in chief who has taken great pride that not a single American soldier has died in battle during his tenure in the White House. Those brave men who died in an Iranian desert were perhaps not killed in a conventional battlefield situation, but they died in battle nonetheless—the battle with an outlaw government to try to free Americans

---

*This essay originally appeared in the Sunday *Atlanta Journal and Constitution*.

kidnapped by barbarians who have to date shown not the slightest degree of respect for international law or custom. It is almost unbelievable how Iranian officials could talk solemnly, with straight faces, about American violation of international law in the failed effort to free Americans from the hands of a kidnapping mob.

The military option has always been an option, as President Carter has made clear. His priority, however, from the beginning has been to seek the freedom of the hostages, to save their lives if at all possible, by doing anything the United States honorably could do in the way of negotiations. Carter has shown the patience of Job in this pursuit and over the past months the slow escalation of pressures and the continued negotiations have again and again seemed tantalizingly close to success.

Some Iranian officials have pretty flatly said that they would like to see the hostages released, that this is a problem that could be solved promptly. The trouble has been, of course, that these officials were not in charge in any command sense, certainly not in command of the terrorists holding the Americans prisoners in our embassy.

Sometimes, the efforts to persuade the terrorists to turn the Americans at least over to the government itself seemed only an inch away from success. The kidnappers each time refused to release their prisoners to anyone.

There are some things a president of the United States could not do in this trying ordeal. It would have been wrong, and dishonorable, for the United States to try to send the shah back to Iran, where our former ally would face certain death. It would be wrong for the president to apologize in some abject fashion for our previous ties with the deposed shah. He was a steady friend in a hard time, and the fanatics who seized power opposed him for the most part because of his progressive ways, such as land reform and women's rights, rather than because of the misdoings of his secret police. The present crowd of barbarians running Iran make the shah look relatively good.

But the shah is not the issue. He is no longer in power and, whatever his sins, he did not kidnap the fifty plus Americans being held in our embassy.

The issue is how you deal with outlaws who hold innocent people captive, often threatening to murder those prisoners if anyone tries to free them.

President Carter has tried patience, negotiations, reason in an effort to win the freedom of those captives. The effort this past week was an attempted rescue operation made only after nothing else seemed to work. The effort failed. We can suffer for the families of the eight brave Americans who died in that attempt, but there is, Lord knows, no reason to be ashamed of them. They are heroes in a genuine sense, all volunteers for a complex, difficult military operation that in the end did not work out.

President Carter took responsibility for the effort that failed, and the responsibility is his. Yet it takes courage to try and the one sure thing is that Carter will continue to try, to undertake whatever in the end must be undertaken to free the Americans being held against their will in Tehran.

Bert Lance's Long Ordeal Ends At Last

May 1, 1980

Bert Lance's long ordeal ended Wednesday as a federal jury found him innocent of bank-fraud charges that have dogged him for more than two years.

There never was any bank fraud involving the former federal budget director, and the flimsy government case evaporated in court when put to some simple, old-fashioned tests, such as producing evidence to support the assorted allegations of Lance's wrongdoing.

Government prosecutors came forward some months ago with an absolute blockbuster of a document declaring Lance's sins. It did not quite state that he once kicked a dog on the streets of Calhoun, or that he had robbed a blind man's cup on Sunday outside church; but just about any banking transaction Lance had ever touched in his banking career was included and alleged in some fashion to be crooked.

There were twenty-two separate counts against Lance at the beginning. The judge and jury either dismissed or completely acquitted Lance on nineteen of the twenty-two. The jurors could not agree on the other three, and the judge declared a mistrial on those. Consider the three. Two counts question financial statements made to banks, one questioned a $12,000 unsecured loan, a loan not repaid because the man borrowing later ran into serious financial troubles. That's all small potatoes indeed when compared to the extravagant government contention at the beginning that there was more than $20 million involved in illegal loans.

Bert Lance survived his long, difficult ordeal with head held high for one clear, simple reason. He knew going in that he was an honest and honorable man, that he had not cheated anybody or misused bank funds in any crooked manner, and his friends and family knew that, too.

The slipshod government case was a disgrace. Justice Department attorneys and investigators spent more than a year investigating Bert Lance, checking out virtually every banking document that had ever passed through any of the banks with which he had been associated. They never found evidence, not a single instance, that Lance had deliberately swindled anyone or any bank. Indeed, one of their weakest points of argument was simply that no bank ever lost money on loans to Lance or to members of his family. They were good loans, with every dime repaid, including interest.

Sometimes investigations take on a life of their own. There is some reason to feel a suspicion that the government attorneys involved in the Lance case persisted in bringing a case in part because they had spent so much time on it. There isn't much glory in working on a complex case for more than a year and then reporting that, well, maybe this is not the kind of case that should be taken to court at all.

The lawyers pushed forward with what is sometimes called the "shotgun" approach, namely throwing everything but the kitchen sink into a long listing of charges on the theory that at least some of those charges might stick; or as the theory sometimes is put, a jury might conclude, with so many charges listed, that they, after all, had to convict Lance of something.

District Judge Charles Moye caught enough flak from both sides during the course of the long trial, but on the whole the judge struggled manfully with a most controversial case. Lance's attorneys at one point asked that the judge disqualify himself, on the ground that he so consistently ruled against their defense motions.

Moye declined to remove himself from the case, and he pushed hard to get a jury verdict on all the charges, without anything left hanging. That was not possible, but it is to the judge's credit that he tried.

The keystone to the prosecution's case was a voluminous count of "conspiracy," alleging that Lance and his three code-fendants had conspired apparently in every way known to man to swindle everybody in sight. There were some 200 separate banking loans or transactions listed in that central part of the charge against Lance. Judge Moye, who had not appeared overly sympathetic to the Lance defense, seemed to become frustrated himself in trying to deal with the supposed evidence for this huge conspiracy charge. He, in effect, asked the government lawyers in court to give him just some modicum of evidence that any "conspiracy" had taken place, anywhere, at any time. There was no such evidence. None. The judge dismissed that lengthy conspiracy account entirely, without even letting those phony-baloney charges go to the jury.

What does an innocent person do when finally found innocent after more than two years of trial by innuendo, trial by news leak, trial by endless allegation (without proof)? Bert Lance will survive because he is a man of considerable character and ability. He will make a new life. But the question needs to be asked: is there no penalty for a prosecution by government on such a flimsy and slipshod basis? Does no one in government have responsibility for the injustices of such a case?

One of poet William Shakespeare's famous passages, from the play *Othello*, reads thus, "Who steals my purse steals trash; 'tis something, nothing; 'Twas mine, 'tis his, and has been slave to thousands; But he that filches from me my good name, Robs me of that which not enriches him, And makes me poor indeed."

Bert Lance will not only survive, he will do well. He will do well because he had not done anything wrong in any serious fashion in the first place. His good name will survive for the same good reason, though there is no way to measure the effect on him and his family of the torturous process of the past two years plus.

Justice? Yes, it was done in the end at the new federal building on Spring Street in Atlanta. But there are people involved in this long, drawn-out case who must answer to their own consciences if to no one else. They must also get up in the morning and look themselves in the face in the mirror. Bert Lance can do that without any problem. Not everyone involved in this case can.

Jimmy Carter
Comes Home
to Georgia

January 20, 1981

Jimmy Carter comes home to Georgia today, a private citizen for the first time in four years. He comes home with honor. His failures were real enough, whether in his attempts to get a handle on the roller-coaster economy of the past two or three years or in the abortive military effort to rescue the American hostages in Iran. His achievements were real too, and the Panama Canal treaties, the normalization of relations with China, the first comprehensive energy program in the nation's history, and the Camp David accords may someday rank Carter a good deal higher in the history books than a majority of American voters ranked him last November.

His greatest failure was the failure successfully to communicate a sense of vision and purpose as president, a sense that he was competent and on top of the job and dealing with the problems as they came along. Those who worked most closely with him in Washington—both those who had known him before and those who came to know him only as president—found him highly intelligent and knowledgeable and decisive. Yet the general perception of Carter, one conveyed sometimes with the help of his friends, was often that of a fellow giving off an uncertain signal, not quite sure of his own direction.

Yet Carter served his country with honor for these four years. That is no small thing in our recent history. Two presidents, Lyndon Johnson and Richard Nixon, were driven from office because they lied to the American people. Johnson lied to us, repeatedly, about the war in Vietnam, and he broke faith on that issue with the people who elected him. Maybe sometimes Johnson believed his own lies, but he simply did not in the end tell us the truth.

Nixon's darker spirit was more sinister than that; he not only lied to us over and over, he was also willing to abuse the powers of the presidency, including using the FBI and the CIA to cover up criminal actions committed by his reelection committee and top staffers. His resignation, the first of an American president in 200 years of our nation, was a low point in the history of the White House. Even Gerald Ford, who in some ways did much to heal the country after Watergate, left a certain sour taint on his tenure with that full pardon of Richard Nixon before Nixon had ever actually been called to account for his violations of law.

Carter served us with honor. Whatever his mistakes there has probably never been a modern president who worked so hard at making himself knowledgeable on issues or tried harder to make decisions that were in the best interest of the country and of the world, all other considerations aside.

His advocacy of "human rights" as part of American values and true values that ought to be part of American foreign policy brought smiles to the faces of some who considered themselves more realistic and tough-minded about the world. Yet ideals and ideas have an impact on the real world too, along with military force and diplomatic niceties. There are people in countries over the world who escaped prison or torture because the United States in this period invoked that concept of human rights and maintained the pressure. Oh, sometimes unevenly, sometimes yielding to diplomatic and geopolitical realities. But it was a continuing theme of American policy while Carter was in the White House because Carter cared about those human rights.

He served us with honor. Welcome home, James Earl.

Part III

Some
Who Made
a Difference

These essays each focus on a single individual and if there is a pattern to them, it is that I perceived each as having great impact on the lives of other people in a positive and decent way.

Some were written about such persons after their deaths, but by no means all. Baseball hero Hank Aaron, labor leader E. L. Abercrombie, Judge George T. Smith, and Coca-Cola philanthropist Robert W. Woodruff were still very much alive and active when the articles about them were written, as were radio newsman Aubrey Morris and former Atlanta Mayor Ivan Allen and educator-extraordinary Benjamin Mays. There was some question as to whether attorney Robert Steed was alive, let alone active, on the occasion when a roast of Colonel Steed was held in Macon. Yet the essay on that event is included for compassionate reasons. Even a failed bond lawyer needs *some* recognition.

For the most part, the columns about persons recently departed were not written in sadness. These people had lived full and fruitful lives and, if there was sadness, there was also the sense of good spirit that such individuals had graced this planet. There were exceptions to this. Allard Lowenstein and Anwar Sadat and Omar Torrijos died violent deaths, and in each case it seemed such a great waste. Each had achieved much, yet each also had the potential of achieving much more.

I recall purposefully writing two essays about individuals facing death within a few days, so that each could read my small tribute while still alive. One, Bernice McCullar, called me on that very day of publication; she seemed gay and cheerful and we chatted about a lot of different things. I did not see Clarence Bacote again before his death, but the column was read to him and gave him great pleasure, his wife told me later. That Bacote essay is included in this section. The initial article on Bernice is not; in its place is a later column written after a tree-planting ceremony in her honor at the state capitol.

One consistent thread in these essays is my own deep belief that a single committed individual can truly make a difference in this world. I expressed this belief about as well as I can in writing about the death of Egyptian President Anwar Sadat:

Those who hold that all of history is shaped totally by mechanical or social forces of some order are idiots, whatever
their academic credentials. They fail to trust their own
hearts, their own spirits, their own individual capacities.
Sure there are, no doubt, forces moving sometimes with historic implications, with the odds against any individual stopping or changing them utterly. But there are the compelling
instances too of individuals who made a huge difference in the
world as it existed. There are the Hitlers and those who create
evil. There are the rare ones, a Sadat, who found the strength
and courage to make peace in a troubled part of the world that
had not known peace in his lifetime.

The individuals portrayed in this section are among those
who made a difference. I knew them all. They enriched my life
and the lives of others.

In Memory
of a Truly
Gentle Man

November 3, 1969[12]

Clarence J. Jordan, a heavyset, gentle man, died last week on Koinonia Farm near Americus. He was buried appropriately, in a pine box in a pasture on the farm, still a part of the integrated Christian community he founded more than twenty-five years ago. It was a controversial community. There's no good explanation for its survival, other than Jordan's character. He was a kindly, soft-spoken man, one who no doubt knew fear from time to time. He must have been afraid sometimes, when through the years the Koinonia community

---

[12]Those who loved Clarence Jordan considered him a huge success, if unconventional. His brother, Robert Jordan, was a success in a quite different way: an active lawyer, influential in politics, appointed first to the Georgia Court of Appeals and then to the Georgia Supreme Court. Sometimes the careers of the two men seemed in conflict. Robert Jordan was a close adviser to Ernest Vandiver, elected governor of Georgia in 1958. Vandiver's opponent in that race denounced Clarence Jordan as a wild-eyed integrationist and attacked Vandiver on the basis that this terrible fellow's brother was Vandiver's adviser. The family ties remained intact. I remember with pleasure the warm and loving letter Robert Jordan wrote me about his brother after this column ran.

became the focal point for beatings and bombings and burnings and an economic boycott. Yet if he worried about himself or his family, it never had the effect of making him run away or give up.

You see, Clarence Jordan got the curious idea in his head that black and white people could live together in the same farm community in a sharing kind of Christian fellowship. It wasn't an idea accepted in the all-white segregated version of Christianity practiced by most white citizens in southwest Georgia. It still isn't.

The racial issue made Koinonia especially controversial, more so in the 1950s after the Supreme Court decision on school segregation than when founded in 1942 (though it was controversial enough then). The word "Koinonia" is a Greek word, meaning fellowship or togetherness.

Jordan and his wife and two small children started the community on 400 acres of land initially, about eight miles southwest of Americus. Jordan said later that he wanted in some way to give himself in service to people in Georgia, principally to rural people, both white and black.

By this time, because of his educational background, he was already a rare combination—a farmer-theologian. He was first a graduate of the University of Georgia, where he studied agriculture. Later, he attended the Southern Baptist Theological Seminary at Louisville, Kentucky, where he received a master's degree in theology and a doctor of philosophy degree in the Greek New Testament. He spent four years with the Baptist Fellowship and city missions in Louisville, working mostly in slum areas, before founding Koinonia Farm.

It was the integration issue that made the community so controversial. But as Mrs. Jordan commented after her husband's death: "Koinonia was never an integrationist movement as people around here thought. Integration is part of the brotherhood of man. Koinonia was Clarence's church."

The farm, after a time, came to specialize in growing pecans and selling them to customers all over the world, though not to local people, who still maintain something close to a 100-per-cent-effective economic boycott.

Jordan was always a student and scholar and, before his death, published what he called "Cotton Patch" translations of parts of the New Testament in an effort, as he put it, "to strip away the fancy language, the artificial piety and barriers of time and distance."

He died of a heart attack last Wednesday, at the age of fifty-seven, just after autographing a copy of his latest book (published only a few days before) for a young girl who lives on Koinonia Farm.

He was buried quietly, as he wished, with no marker on the grave, still wearing the blue jeans and red plaid shirt in which he liked to walk around the farm.

He lived in Georgia all his life, and he'll be remembered by many people: a remarkable man, who loved all men whatever their circumstances or skin color. A gentle man, who yet became involved in bombings and beatings and the fierce social issues of a troubled era. He never wavered in his beliefs. Though a soft-spoken gentleman, there's a comment someone made once about Ralph McGill, late publisher of the *Atlanta Constitution*, which also applies to Clarence Jordan: simply that "he had guts when it *took* guts to have guts."

Jordan was a strong and idealistic and decent man. He will be remembered.

Ivan Allen:
Unlikely Catalyst
of Social Change

December 11, 1969

The architects of dynamic social change in this nation come in varied shapes and sizes.

A Catholic priest in Milwaukee, with a terrible intensity and the burning eyes of a fanatic . . . or a saint. A young black minister, with brains and heart, who only a little over a decade ago was unknown, but whose vision came to dominate the movement toward racial justice in the country and whose clear baritone voice would ring out into history as he voiced his belief in this country . . . *I have a dream.*

Yes, the people who shape social change come in unlikely forms. Like Mayor Ivan Allen, who looks like what he is, a successful businessman, a man likely to be at home with boards of directors or taking his turn as president of any civic club whose members are relatively affluent.

Mayor Allen, whose eight years in office will end in another month, shaped this city as much as any man ever has (other, maybe, than Gen. Sherman and those other unruly Yankee-types who burned it down).

He influenced it, primarily, because when the terrible storm of racial controversies erupted at the beginning of this decade, he had vision enough to understand more than most of his contemporaries. And he had the courage to take the razor-edge of such controversy in hand, to refuse to pretend that it would all go away if we shut our eyes tightly enough, and to take action.

It's a sign of how rapidly things have changed (though no one can pretend that problems have all been solved) that when Ivan Allen was thinking about running for mayor the first time, back in 1961, at that stage the crucial racial question in Georgia was whether or not to close down the entire public school system, rather than desegregate the schools. It's not likely that any public official would even mention such a possibility today.

Allen appeared the other day at the Atlanta Press Club, a kind of sentimental journey, in a way, a kind of talking to the same press people who have been sympathetic to what he was trying to do in the past eight (or almost eight) years.

In terms of his first year or so in office, says Mayor Allen, no doubt quite accurately, "I was encompassed in everything I did with civil rights problems." Allen said, too, "Every third person who walked into the office was a delegation from the transition areas, wanting to know what could be done. . . ."

Again, it's hard to realize in this day and time just how difficult such things were. The young people, in particular, those now in college or just after, simply do not understand. What they fail to grasp is just that there were tough battles to fight before they were old enough to vote . . . to be drafted.

After the sit-ins began, Mayor Allen grasped, as did few white men in the South, that we were talking about revolution. Genuine social revolution.

As the good high mayor put it, "Atlanta was beginning to feel its omissions. . . ." It was a time when the sit-ins, in truth, were dominating the political life of the South. As Mayor Allen described what was going on, there were dozens of young civil rights demonstrators all breaking the law and choosing to remain in jail. "They didn't want to come out of jail . . . they just wanted to sit there and sing 'We Shall Overcome' and make a national impact," Allen said.

The thing of it is, folks, that most of us may face in one fashion or the other the difficult issues of our own time. There are a few people . . . there aren't many . . . but a few, who have the perception and the sheer tough-minded courage of it, to react to the meanest—and toughest—social issues of an era, and to react and act with decency and good sense.

A Memory
of Brandy
and Paris

August 14, 1971

TRENTON NJ—This gets around in a moment to Atlanta
and what people sometimes say or think about this singular
city. The moment-in-waiting is for a gentleman who died the
other day, named Robert Gulliver, a favorite uncle of mine and
the reason I was in Trenton.

He was a gentle, sweet man, despite passing much of the
time as a Connecticut-born, conservative New England Republican (which he was), or as a stern-eyed, quite efficient certified public accountant, which he also was.

Oh, those were poses, of course. Withal, he had perhaps the
most gentle, slight, sweet smile of any man I've ever known. If
that sounds sentimental, gentle reader, I can only submit that
you never saw him smile.

He hated television. Couldn't stand it. His wife, Alta, loved
it. Loved watching sporting events. He never said a word. They
could sit in the same room, she watching, say, a golf tourna-
ment on television, he sitting quite deliberately with his back
to the TV set and reading the *New York Times.*

He never objected. But when, at the end of a televised sports event, she would walk over and switch off the set, he would speak aloud, perhaps not looking up from his newspaper. "Thank you," he would say.

He adored his wife. Spoiled her in many ways, probably. Remained absolutely devoted to one woman for better than fifty years. No doubt an old-fashioned and semiobsolete trait in this modern world.

She died a few months ago. He, nearly eighty-one, was not in bad health, but also was not very strong. The nursing home was a good one. Up until the end, he drank a small glass of wine before lunch each day, one gin-and-tonic just before dinner. Occasionally he bought a lottery ticket in the now-legal state sweepstakes; protested to one friend that he felt sure he'd had a winning ticket over the past several months but couldn't quite pin the number down on any of the lists. When he died, it was very quick and peaceful, and I suspect that slight, sweet smile was on his face.

Once, when I was a good deal younger and the world seemed mine, I was a student at the Free University in West Berlin and that September my uncle and aunt flew to Paris for a long-awaited European vacation. They sent me an airline ticket and insisted I fly to Paris to join them. It was my twenty-second birthday, and my Uncle Bob was resolved that we toast that occasion in rare brandy. But it was late evening, and the only way to do what he wanted was to purchase an entire bottle of expensive brandy from the hotel bar at by-the-drink prices.

Probably a silly thing to remember, but that bottle of brandy cost more than you would believe offhand. My uncle and aunt and I had, it being late, no more than one small glass apiece. It wasn't the money or the brandy, but just that it was important to him that we toast a birthday in appropriate style.

Back to Atlanta. After the funeral, a man from New York asked me why people kept saying Atlanta was such an exciting city. A lady who teaches at an upper New York State college said the female coeds talk now of moving to Atlanta to live and work as they once talked of moving to San Francisco.

Occurs to me that this column is not very much about Atlanta, mostly about my late Uncle Bob. That's all right. He was worth mourning.

Two Stories:
Bobby Jones
and Ralph Bunche

December 23, 1971

The people who died aren't far ahead of the rest of us; we'll all go that way. Not much choice, is there?

So, when you consider these things, in a way, it's not the dying or the talking about dying, but more the style of living and dying.

Let's talk about Bobby Jones. Superb athlete, golfer, all that. Made that Grand Slam, did well. Right?

Also, from all reports, a genuinely nice guy. A man who, along with his athletic abilities, made a serious, successful career in later years as a lawyer and businessman. Can you believe he retired from his first career at the age of twenty-eight? After winning all the awards there were to win in his chosen sport, amateur or professional.

Atlanta attorney Henry Troutman said once, quoting a doctor, that there were only three certainties about death. First of all, you're going to die. Everyone is. Secondly, you probably will never know in advance exactly when you will die. And, last of all, you likely never will be sure ahead of time exactly what will kill you.

Those things are generally true for all of us. Not entirely, in all cases. Bobby Jones may not have known the day and the hour, but he battled for years against the effects of a progressively crippling disease. And he knew, no doubt, that one day it would finally kill him.

This gets around to a small Bobby Jones story. There are many, but I like this one. It ought to be written down somewhere.

Friend of mine was in an Atlanta building one day, starting from an office along a corridor to an elevator, when he recognized Bobby Jones ahead of him, waiting for the elevator. After disease struck him, Jones first began to use a single walking cane. Later, he used two canes, and still later he was in a wheelchair. This was at the first stage, with one cane, though Jones's back was already somewhat twisted.

Jones was standing there, leaning on the one cane. There was no one in sight, and he apparently thought he was quite alone, not seeing the man approaching from behind him. Suddenly, Jones turned the cane upside down and pretended it was a golf club, taking a practice swing and . . . who knows? . . . maybe remembering how the green looked at St. Andrews. The other man hesitated, waiting a tactful minute, not wanting to let Jones know he had been seen at his harmless imaginary game.

People remember their contacts, even though brief ones, with distinguished persons. This next one has no connection with Bobby Jones, but it is a nice, small story about another famous man, recently deceased, Ralph Bunche. Bunche, who rose to international prominence through his United Nations role, was in Atlanta not long after he had put together the 1949 peace settlement in the Middle East, a feat that won him the Nobel Peace Prize.

One Atlantan remembers asking him about the tense, round-the-clock negotiating session at the very end, when it looked as if Arab and Jewish spokesmen simply would not agree. The Atlantan asked, what were you thinking about all that time?

Bunche's eyes twinkled and he smiled. Do you really want to know? he asked. Yes, of course, he was told. Well, Bunche said, special gift pottery had been made up for the dozens of participants in the negotiations. At the very end, when it looked as if no agreement could be worked out, said Bunche: "I kept thinking how I was going to be stuck with all that damned pottery."

For Him,
No Sadness
of Farewell

January 27, 1976

VALDOSTA GA—Doctor Gulliver would have enjoyed his funeral, a woman said to me on the day we buried my father, and I thought about it later and decided that was probably right.

The woman who made the remark was the wife of a boyhood friend of mine, Ernest McDonald, whose family has lived next door to mine for the last thirty years and more. The McDonalds have always been good neighbors. My father's health failed in the last couple of years, his feet became uncertain. He had several bad falls, sometimes in the middle of the night, probably on his way to the bathroom. Mr. McDonald, Ernest's father, has more than once gotten out of bed on a moment's notice to hurry next door and help my mother lift my father and place him back into bed. In a way, nothing touched me more at the graveyard services than the glimpse of Mr. McDonald's face as he passed, face squinched up, eyes blinking, face full of hurt; he seemed about to cry.

But funerals ought not to be too sad, not for someone who has lived a long and full and good life, and at eighty-two my father had done that.

He would have enjoyed the funeral. There were old friends there, some he had not seen in a while, lovely flowers and music, and poetry too. He taught English literature for more than forty years and loved Shakespeare best, and then Robert Browning and Robert Frost and a host of others. He liked his own poetry too and one of the mild few regrets of his life was, as he put it, that he was only a minor, minor poet; he would have loved being one of the great ones. He approved of the Episcopal burial services; indeed, he was still technically a member of Christ Church in New Haven, and he would have especially liked it that three short poems of his own (minor poet or not) were read just before the burial services began.

My father broke out of the New England snows more than four decades ago, left Yale to take his chances teaching in deep South Georgia. It became his home: he never looked back or thought of living anywhere else, and he would have especially valued the tribute in the *Valdosta Times*, which ended this way:

> But most of all, Dr. Gulliver loved people. His infectious smile was constant and genuine. He always had an encouraging word to students and a good word for friends.
>
> He came here as a stranger, a Yankee used to cities and happenings, and he made himself one of us—made our town, our college and all of us, better because of his life.

It is true. He would have enjoyed the funeral, no doubt about that. He would have been of good cheer and wanted his friends to be and to pay attention to Tennyson's poem, "Crossing the Bar," read at the graveside service, especially the third stanza:

> *Twilight and evening bell,*
> *And after that the dark!*
> *And may there be no sadness of farewell,*
> *When I embark.*

Bernice McCullar
and Her Dogwood
at the Capitol

April 6, 1976

It was a nice occasion. There is something pleasant about planting a tree, or in this case dedicating the dogwood planted at one corner of the state capitol grounds in memory of Bernice Brown McCullar.

Bernice died not long ago, shortly after she had retired from the state capitol complex, where for years she worked as information officer or whatever her title was at the State Department of Education. That job title, even if stated accurately, wouldn't give anyone much notion of Bernice and what admiration and affection she routinely drew from those who knew her.

She was fascinated with education and learning all her life, loved books and people, and had rather a gift for words and rather a knack for friendship.

Most journalists covering the state capitol got to know her and came pretty quickly to understand that on any given day, likely as not, Bernice had more sense and judgment about what was going on in state government than anyone else around. She was helpful and shrewd and always candid when asked a question, even when the answer might not necessarily aid the cause of her department of state government. She understood that journalists can forgive a lot of things; being lied to is not one of them.

It was a nice occasion. Steve Polk, the able director of the Georgia Building Authority, helped pick out the little dogwood tree. It is called a "Cloud Nine," he said, a new hybrid variety that he thought is considered a superior one and therefore "appropriate for Miss Bernice."

There was poetry, and a proclamation from Gov. George Busbee making it Bernice McCullar Day in Georgia, and a brief, responsive reading by the several dozen people there dedicating the tree to Bernice.

There was some family there, her daughter from Texas, and it was curious. The date for the dedication of the dogwood tree had only been set a few days ago, and there had been efforts made to get in touch with Bernice's daughter; but no one had been able to make contact, because it turned out the daughter and her family were on vacation, traveling about. Purely by chance, they were in Georgia this morning and yesterday morning and saw an item in the paper with the time and place and got to the state capitol in time to take part in the dedication ceremony.

Once, years ago, while Bernice's late husband was still alive, a governor of Georgia wanted to appoint him to a public office and then ran into some difficulties with getting the appointment approved. Finally, when it looked as if it could not be made to work out, the governor called Bernice and said her husband had some enemies and the appointment would not go through. But, the governor added, he would willingly nominate Bernice for the post and could get that approved. It must have been a temptation, at least for a moment, for a spirited and competent and intelligent woman. But she was a wise woman too and could understand at once how that would make her husband feel, and she gently told the governor no.

Ah, well. It was a clear, sunny, altogether beautiful day, a nice day to be alive and yet a nice day to think of an old friend and help dedicate a dogwood tree. Bernice would have thought it all appropriate and delightful and would have liked thinking about that dogwood tree growing at that corner of the state capitol for years to come.

Dr. Benjamin Mays Is a Real Hero

September 21, 1977

Dr. Benjamin Mays was eighty-three years young this summer, and his abiding intelligence and quick mind belie that would-be verdict of the decades.

He shrugs off decades in the proverbial fashion of water from a duck's back; and at an age when most people seek more restful avocations, Mays is running for a new four-year term as president of the Atlanta School Board, campaigning actively against his two opponents (one of whom is a lady he always mentions with respect, noting that her husband has been a friend of his for many years).

Mays will win a new term almost surely. That is not even offered as a prediction, but rather simply as an acknowledgment of the admiration generally felt for Dr. Mays in both white and black communities in Atlanta. A more serious question might be, why should a man with such a clear head and abundant energy, even at age eighty-three, want to spend his time dealing with the thorny problems of an urban public school system? Be grateful that he cares, and that is probably as complete an answer as there is.

Mays grew up in what some call the "white man's South," a hard time for any black person, let alone one of great gifts, bright enough to understand the injustices of racism at an early age, and yet living in a time long before the civil rights revolution. He was thus doubly frustrated by an understanding of racial injustice, but without being able reasonably to contemplate a time when such segregated patterns would change.

One of Mays's earliest memories came when he was only four years old and a crowd of white night riders caught up with him and his father and cussed his father, pointing their guns at him and making him take off his hat and bow down several times. In later life Mays came to understand that this particular mob was one associated with what was called the Phoenix Riot, which began in Greenwood County in South Carolina on November 8, 1898, and included the lynching of several black persons in the several days following.

Yet Mays, always a religious person, believed firmly even from those frightening early times that hard work and faith and education were capable of elevating anyone, black or white, to levels of solid achievement. He became an educator and his achievements through the years are too numerous to list, many coming in the period of the 1940s and 1950s and 1960s while he served as president of Morehouse College in the Atlanta University complex. There is little doubt that his continuing dedication to education and to the opportunities that education can mean for young people springs directly from his own experience. Atlanta is certainly the gainer because of a fellow like Benjamin Mays who still cares enough to want the Atlanta public schools to be places of opportunity.

Oh, he has some detractors. He does not think, for one thing, that unions have a right to run the Atlanta school system, insisting on the quaint notion that maybe the members of the school board (elected by Atlanta citizens after all) and school officials ought to make major and significant decisions. An even greater sin, he has been accused of nodding drowsily in school board meetings; anyone who has ever been to a prolonged school board meeting may well sympathize.

But his achievements are significant and long-term. He was part of putting together a school desegregation plan for Atlanta four years ago, which was acceptable both to the white and black community and also to the federal courts.

Some civil rights leaders blasted Mays and other Atlantans for agreeing to any sort of plan that did not involve extensive busing back and forth over the city. Mays wanted Atlanta schools integrated, of course, but he also wanted white and black pupils alike to remain within the school system and he wanted quality education for all pupils with as little disruption as possible. He took the heat of some criticism because he cared enough about the pupils actually involved in the school system itself.

Anyway, in what often seems an unheroic time, it is nice to have a few real heroes around. Benjamin Mays is one.

On Remembering
Savannah's
Pinkie Masters

November 16, 1977

They buried Pinkie Masters in Savannah yesterday, and his mourners were a motley crew, ranging from the occasional stray journalist or college student or blue-collar worker to the president of the United States.

All remembered Pinkie fondly, as a rule remembered having a drink in his small, friendly tavern just across from the DeSoto Hilton Hotel. It was a gathering spot, that tavern. The conglomerations of people that filled it up on occasion were enough to boggle the mind.

There was a warm summer evening just over two years ago now, and the crowd in Pinkie's that night ran rather to lawyers and judges. There were two Georgia Supreme Court judges there, with their wives, and an appellate court judge behind the bar mixing drinks. The appellate court judge, as it happened, did not even drink, but the place was a little crowded and busy and he took great relish in tending bar for a bit, lending Pinkie a hand.

Pinkie Masters was a feisty, colorful, outgoing man of Greek descent, born Louis Christopher Masterpolis. Despite that ethnic background, his tavern became virtually the center of Savannah's irrepressible St. Patrick's Day celebration each year. "I may be Greek," he would say, "but on St. Patrick's Day I am the biggest Irishman in the world."

He was good with people, good at remembering names, seemed as a rule to enjoy his tavern more than any customer, and maybe that liking of people was what got him involved in politics. Oh, and he was feisty about it. Sometimes he was with winners, and sometimes he was with losing candidates, and he would just about fight with you in declaring the virtues of his particular candidate. Far as I know, he never wanted anything from anybody, though he helped elect several governors and a congressman and, yes, a president of the United States. Nothing, that is, except for the candidate to be a good candidate or the officeholder to do a good job. Once, he got mad at a candidate who couldn't remember names; somebody had contributed $1,000 to the candidate and the candidate couldn't remember the name of the contributor. That wasn't good politics at all, Pinkie knew, and it made him mad.

Maybe he liked underdogs in his politics, because he didn't try to go with the tide and the sure favorites. He was for Carl Sanders the first time Sanders ran, when Sanders definitely started out as an underdog and yet won, and then was for Jimmy Carter in 1970, when Carter appeared the underdog. Carter as governor dropped in at Pinkie's pub, even took a turn at tending bar. "He's an awful bartender. He's always spilling the drinks," he said about Carter once.

If memory serves, Pinkie got mad at Carter about something or other while Carter was governor and, as always, Pinkie spoke his views plainly. But by the time Carter's term as governor was over and the Georgian was running for president, Pinkie was back on his side again, intrigued maybe by the underdog effort of all time. Early in the national campaign, when few Georgians even took Carter seriously, Pinkie had set aside a little room next to his tavern where he worked until all hours of the night handlettering "Jimmy Carter for President" signs.

Carter remembered his old friend after becoming president and knew that Pinkie was ill and called him from the White House more than once, the last time being last Sunday night. He had passed on only minutes before.

Well, Pinkie would like being mourned in the White House, probably, as he certainly is. But he would like equally being remembered by the literally thousands of people who dropped in at his tavern at sometime or other and found it a place full of warmth and good humor and friendly talk. And he will be.

How Aubrey Morris Shut the City Down

January 13, 1978

Governors and mayors and school officials are often under the illusion that they control things, oh say, like shutting down office buildings and school systems in the event of snow and ice storms.

But it is worth noting that there was a day when one Aubrey Morris, he of the slightly nasal voice and ubiquitous mien, shut down Atlanta tighter than anyone ever had; and there really was not a snowstorm at all, only, as the legend has had it ever since, three or four snowflakes in Aubrey's front yard.

You do not hear the distinctive Morris voice on WSB radio these days in the constant fashion of a while ago. Morris has risen to be some kind of High-Muckety-Muck executive and he spends his time doing whatever it is High-Muckety-Mucks do.

Yet he used to be an honest-to-goodness reporter, as opposed to merely a High-Muckety-Muck, and it was in those palmy days that Morris shut Atlanta down.

William Hartsfield was mayor of Atlanta then, and before the day was over he was telephoning WSB radio and demanding of all the High-Muckety-Mucks of that time, what in the world gave Aubrey Morris the authority to shut the city down? That was what mayors were supposed to do.

As Morris recalled it yesterday, sitting in his current High-Muckety-Muck office at WSB, he at the time was the one-man news department at the radio station and had early duty that morning, so early that he was starting out of his driveway onto an icy street at 4 A.M. "I'll never make it to the station," Morris remembers saying to himself, as he inched along the treacherous street.

He got to an intersection and saw a police car sliding around just as he was, and he stopped and got out and conferred with the police captain. Morris and the police captain both gave up their cars and went to a nearby home and commandeered a telephone, and Morris began broadcasting from there.

It was the police captain, Morris insists, who started saying, please, everybody stay home, there is no way to drive on these streets. But it was that distinctive Aubrey Morris voice that most people remember as they rolled out of bed early in the day and were told, forget it, there was no way to get to the city that day.

That police captain's car had been "skidding around like a mosquito on a south Georgia pond," recalled Morris, and for a couple of early morning hours the streets were apparently bad indeed. Morris finally started trying to drive to the station again, broadcasting as he went, and at one point he saw a man careening out of a driveway and knew there was about to be an accident.

He described the car and announced on the radio, "I am about to be hit," and his listeners got an on-the-scene report of his being hit. The man who hit him, in fact, had his radio on and was listening to Aubrey describe the accident just before it happened.

Well, most everybody stayed home, except Morris and Mayor Hartsfield, and then naturally by midmorning the sun was out and warm and by noon the streets were fine. But the schools and city offices and downtown stores were still closed.

That's the kind of influence Aubrey Morris had before he became a High-Muckety-Muck.

Anonymous Donor Strikes Yet Again

September 13, 1978[13]

The anonymous donor strikes yet again!

Someone told the story a few years ago. There was a fund-raising effort for some major civic venture, and Robert W. Woodruff was shown a list of people and corporations already signed on to make contributions. Towards the end of the list was an "anonymous donor" who had pledged $50,000. Woodruff supposedly shook his head in puzzlement and observed that he had not yet committed any money for the project.

Woodruff in that particular case was not the anonymous one pledging the $50,000, but his comment was hardly vainglory.

He has been the most generous and best-known anonymous benefactor in Atlanta for decades now, and until only a couple of years ago Woodruff was at considerable pains not to let his name be used in any public fashion. Needless to say,

---

[13]It's worth noting that Woodruff continued his habit of generous giving after this column appeared, including one mind-boggling gift of 100 million dollars to Emory University.

though, his efforts were so generous in so many directions, in millions and millions of dollars, that a certain number of civic leaders knew without any doubt who that phrase meant, the "anonymous donor."

Woodruff built his personal fortune and the Coca-Cola Company at the same time. His generous gifts, since he became wealthy, have lifted spirits and helped people in various ways—people who in many cases never knew the source of the gift that made certain things possible.

Earlier this month, the anonymous donor struck again, this time with a $7 million gift towards the $13 million needed for the proposed new library at the Atlanta University Center. The AU Center has historically served mostly black students and Woodruff expressed confidence "that assurance of the new library as the academic heart of the six institutions is the most effective way I can demonstrate the importance of educational opportunity for all our citizens."

It comes to mind, though, for another reason. Boisfeuillet Jones has for some while supervised the five foundations that Woodruff set up to make various donations, and had some interesting comments about those donations. A couple of years ago, Jones would not have felt free to talk about it all publicly, but that changed some when people insisted on honoring Woodruff publicly for some of the things he had made possible.

Consider some of these remarkable figures. Over the years, Jones said in a civic club speech, the Woodruff foundations have given away more than $250 million, mostly in Atlanta and Georgia. Some of the projects known to have been helped enormously include the Atlanta Memorial Arts Center, the Emory University Medical Center (the Woodruff funding helped make this one of the best in the world), and downtown Central City Park. There have been countless others.

The creation of Central City Park has always in some ways been my favorite Woodruff story. He bought up for roughly $9 million a block right smack in the middle of the city and turned it over to the city to become a refreshing island of small hills and trees and greenery in the heart of Atlanta. That took class.

Jones put it very well when he said that over the years Woodruff's gifts have had genuine impact on the quality of life in Atlanta and the South. The most Anonymous Donor of them all deserves a considerable amount of nonanonymous appreciation.

Aaron
Is a Hit
with Inmates

December 22, 1978

REIDSVILLE—It was an unexpected place for anyone to meet baseball slugger Hank Aaron, along Death Row, but the lean young man did not seem surprised as he looked up from his card game.

"I play for the Yankees," he said, smiling, and pointing at the Yankee baseball cap on his head. That got a grin from Aaron as he moved along the Death Row cells, stopping to shake hands or chat for a moment with anyone interested in meeting the fellow who broke Babe Ruth's home-run record.

One of the men here under sentence of death moved eagerly over to the bars saying, "I never shook the hand of a real hero before."

Aaron spent most of one of the last shopping days before Christmas at this huge state prison facility, touring every wing and cellblock and shaking hands and just saying Merry Christmas. One reason for low attendance at some Atlanta Braves games became clear; there are a lot of Brave fans here who find it difficult, so to speak, to get to Atlanta-Fulton County Stadium these days.

What about pitching? Aaron was asked again and again, along with getting a fair share of baseball advice. "You're going to have to grow some pitchers," said one man. "Nobody is going to trade you a good one," another inmate offered. "Any time somebody trades a pitcher, something is wrong with him."

There were some inmates who said they had seen Aaron's record-breaking 715th home run and one said he had lived near Aaron's neighborhood in Atlanta. It is nothing new for Hank Aaron to sign autographs, but he certainly signed his share Thursday, moving from one cellblock dormitory to another.

He got a little grim about the prison surroundings while walking down the corridors between cellblocks. "I wish every juvenile who gets in a little trouble could be brought here for a tour," Aaron said. But he was full of good humor and good cheer when actually talking to inmates.

The talk got around to the Atlanta Falcons as well as the Atlanta Braves, and Aaron urged some inmates to cross their fingers for the Falcons in this Sunday's playoff game.

There was one man, not really too elderly, who said he had first come to Reidsville in 1945. He had been out of prison a couple of times, but always found his way in one fashion or the other back to Reidsville. There was another who said he had been here for sixteen years and expected to go free in one more year. He was from New Orleans and he and Aaron agreed on the good food and good cooking to be found there.

There was no huge purpose in Aaron's visit, other than just what it seemed, letting a celebrity as well known as Hammerin' Hank tour the prison and shake hands with inmates and say Merry Christmas. It was a nice idea. Gov. George Busbee's office set it up, also arranging an afternoon program of music and other entertainment for several hundred inmates, a program that included a musical group, the Sunshine Express, Pokkets the Clown, and members of the Ben Hill United Methodist Church Choir in Atlanta.

Hank Aaron and the other people taking part in the program spread a good amount of Christmas cheer for a few hours in this prison facility, yet it is hardly the most cheering place to be several days before Christmas. One young man stopped me when he realized I was from a newspaper. He asked that his name, Richard Earl Smith, be mentioned somewhere with a request, maybe, that his mother might write him. His mother is in Atlanta or Georgia, he thinks, though he is not absolutely sure, and he has not heard from her for a long while.

Helen
Did It
Her Way

July 22, 1979

Ol' Blue Eyes, Frank Sinatra, and the ubiquitous Helen Bullard had at least one deepset belief in common.

Sinatra at one stage of his career made his recording of the song, "I Did It My Way," and it stood as something of a personal theme song. Helen liked that song and paid attention to the words. She felt that same theme, that the song might well be hers. She did it her way.

Helen Bullard died last week at the age of seventy-two, after seventy-two years of feisty, caring spirit, during a time when she made the city of Atlanta her own and helped run her city in ways that most people never understood. Oh, she did it her way, no doubt. Consult with any of the dozens and dozens of candidates for public office, most successful, some not, whom she advised over the years.

She specialized maybe in mayors of Atlanta, in that nobody probably was closer as an adviser to the late Mayor Bill Hartsfield, mayor of Atlanta for three decades. Mayor Ivan Allen, Jr. succeeded Hartsfield for two terms through most of the 1960s and Ms. Bullard was close to Allen too. But the mayors part of

her career was only a part; she probably advised as many as-
piring candidates for city council or county commission posts
or congress or statewide office as anyone ever has in Georgia.

Helen pretty much had to decide on her own that she liked
a particular candidate before getting involved, but she could
make judgments, tough judgments, too, sometimes. She did
not care for idiots or racists. She was a white woman who believed in civil rights a long time before it became fashionable
and she never wavered in those kinds of beliefs.

She did not care for idiots, but she had great sympathy for
would-be candidates who seemed pretty decent and interested
in public service of some kind, but who just did not understand
much about politics and government. She was patience itself
(though otherwise often an impatient lady) in trying to explain the ins and outs of the political corridors to some fledgling (though the fledgling might be someone otherwise
distinguished in whatever fashion, just not very knowledgeable about politics).

She also learned things in the process. Once, a candidate
for office walked over to the window and began talking to
Helen about how hard the campaign was, how demanding the
schedule, how difficult for a family, how lengthy the days, and
how sometimes dull the opportunities. It opened her eyes in a
fashion. Oh, she knew those things, but she said later she had
never fully weighed the price just of seeking public office, the
personal demands, the cost in time, and the drain of the experience on anyone who really had never been involved before
in a political campaign.

She came later to speak often about that price. We all, most
of us, talk about getting good people to seek public office.
Helen came to understand just how much we require of those
same good people when they once get into a campaign. There
is, as a rule, never a guarantee. The voters are fickle, and it is
not always true, needless to say, that the best man or woman
wins. Helen came to see what a considerable sacrifice we ask of
those "good people" who do run for public office, even if they
win, let alone if they put forth that considerable effort and then
do not win.

She cared about Atlanta the way a collector might take a fine piece of jade and touch it carefully and lovingly, thinking long and dreamy thoughts. She was a dreamer, this one, a lover of the best in other people, disappointed a little if they failed of that best, yet almost always compassionate at the same time. Bright as a new dime. Tough as an old wooden hickory bucket. Full of fun and joy at anyone's witty turn of phrase, delighted at anyone's small human story of something good that occurred.

She was quite a gal, this Helen. And she really did do it her way.

Allard Lowenstein Was the "Original Activist"

March 19, 1980

NEW YORK—God knows Allard Lowenstein did not intend to be here. Not at Central Synagogue. Not even with so many old friends gathered around, though he would have liked that part.

Lowenstein would have been quick to tell you he had too much yet to do, to be dead at fifty-one; too many causes, too many roads to explore, too many songs unsung. He touched nerves. Made folk worry about what was good for the country. What was honest. What was compassionate.

Lowenstein made them understand. He tried to be understanding himself. To be the quiet moderator. The negotiator. The friend trying to make sense, whether in the civil rights struggles of the 1960s or the Vietnam War. The Rhodesian elections. The unchanging concerns for individual human rights.

That killed him, in a way. A man who once worked with Lowenstein in the civil rights movement came to see him last Friday. Lowenstein knew the man had mental problems, that he had been something of a social dropout, that he insisted people (the CIA included) were out to get him, that most other old friends refused to have anything to do with him. Lowenstein would befriend anyone. Would try to understand. The man shot him five times.

Somebody once called Lowenstein the "original activist," and that is not a bad designation. But his genius was that he believed in the miracle of the American democratic process and that it could be made to work.

He was national student chairman for Adlai Stevenson in the 1952 presidential campaign, one of the first active civil rights leaders in the early 1960s, and one of the first Americans to speak out against the Vietnam War.

It was Lowenstein's help in organizing New Hampshire in 1968 as much as any single factor that forced President Lyndon Johnson to withdraw from that year's presidential race. After he couldn't get his close friend, the late Sen. Robert Kennedy, to run for president, Lowenstein persuaded Sen. Eugene McCarthy to run instead. Later, Johnson withdrew from the race.

Lowenstein remained loyal to McCarthy, but there's an interesting footnote. Robert Kennedy had asked an aide to place a telephone call to Lowenstein shortly before his death on the night of the California primary in 1968. Kennedy had been shot down by the time the call was completed and that was how Lowenstein first learned of the incident.

He spent one term in Congress and served in the United Nations Mission during the first part of President Carter's administration, although Lowenstein was actively supporting Sen. Ted Kennedy in the 1980 campaign.

But those public offices barely begin to suggest the extent of Lowenstein's contacts and influence for more than two decades. The crowds of people who mourned him Tuesday at Central Synagogue give a hint. The 1,200 seats inside were filled long before the services began and another 600 people crowded onto 55th Street to stand in the cold and listen to the memorial services over a speaker.

Sen. Kennedy spoke. New York Gov. Hugh Carey, Sen. Patrick Moynihan, New York Mayor Ed Koch, and Coretta King were there. The range of friendships formed by Lowenstein over the years, however, might be best suggested by two who made remarks at the services: former United Nations Ambassador Andrew Young and columnist William Buckley.

One speaker quoted the late Supreme Court Justice Oliver Wendell Holmes, observing that a man who separated himself from the action and passion of his time ran the peril of being judged not fully to have lived.

Lowenstein was part of both the actions and passions of his era as few have ever been. He was an idealist. A practical politician, one who hated injustice, yet never seemed to hate individual human beings, and one who almost always in a hundred different causes made a difference. That was perhaps the bedrock of his conviction that a single individual could indeed make a difference.

Atlanta Mayor Maynard Jackson knew Lowenstein and recalls a conversation after Lowenstein had been gerrymandered out of his original congressional district and lost several efforts to win reelection.

Someone chided Lowenstein, saying that if he had just modified his outspoken views somewhat, he might have been elected in the new district. Lowenstein smiled and agreed, yet added, "But then I would not have been free."

Lowenstein was that rare commodity: a free man. He fought a hundred losing causes, probably never regretting a single one, and he loved his friends with a remarkable consistency and sense of caring.

On Hanging
George T. Smith
in the Capitol

May 12, 1980[14]

There will be a hanging at the state capitol today. Some folk who have known him for a long time might even wish the hanging were for real, but it will only be a portrait of a man. It is unusual, though, to unveil a portrait of a man still considered among the politically living. If, that is, you can call a judge among the politically living. Some might dispute that point.

In any case, there will be a good crowd on hand to honor State Court of Appeals Judge George T. Smith Monday as his portrait indeed is unveiled under the gold dome of the state capitol.

There is a historical reason. Somebody over there in state government figured out that George T. was apparently unique in Georgia history in being elected at various times to high offices in each of the three major branches of state government:

---

[14]Judge Smith was serving on the State Court of Appeals when this was written. He ran successfully in the fall of 1980 for a seat on the Georgia Supreme Court.

executive, legislative, and judicial. Take them in the order in this case that they happened to fall in Smith's rather varied career.

He was practicing law in Cairo, in Grady County, in deep southwest Georgia, when first elected to the Georgia House in the late 1950s. In 1962 Smith signed on to try to help a brash young state senator run for governor, fellow named Carl Sanders who confounded a great many people by getting elected governor—the first Georgia governor, in fact, elected under a real popular vote after the courts threw out the old county-unit system.

Now, for a mild-mannered sort, Smith has always seemed to make his share of fierce political enemies and it was so in this case. Sanders's major opponent in that race, former Gov. Marvin Griffin, was from that same part of the state and his partisans were rather bitter that George T. had actively supported the man who won. Their feelings were not eased when Smith became Speaker of the Georgia House, this at a time when the House Speaker was, in effect, named by the governor. Incoming Gov. Sanders wanted an ally in that position.

Smith's enemies tried to drum up opposition to him in his home county two years later, hoping to embarrass the governor and Smith too with a defeat. Nothing much came of that. There was something to be said for the old days when a governor ran state government pretty thoroughly.

Four years after laboring in those political vineyards to help elect a governor, Speaker Smith ran for lieutenant governor of Georgia against the incumbent, Lt. Gov. Peter Zack Geer. Geer was the overwhelming favorite and indeed got forty-nine percent plus of the votes the first time around. In Georgia the patterns of voting, however, have not been kind to incumbents who failed to win on the first ballot. Geer, suddenly perceived as being vulnerable by his own enemies and George T.'s friends, could not pull it out in the runoff.

Smith went on to serve four years as lieutenant governor, losing a reelection bid to then-Gov. Lester Maddox. He lost a bid for governor, too, a bit later, but he never learned how to quit and he has loved the political life with some depth and understanding; so the next thing you knew, George T. Smith was running for appellate court judge. He won not simply because of old political ties, but because he had come to be widely respected by most of those who had ever known him, including the state's lawyers, who as a rule play a decisive influence in electing judges.

They will be hanging George T. Smith today over at the state capitol. He probably will enjoy it.

Remembering
Dean Tate
of Georgia

September 24, 1980

This gets around in a moment to William Tate, the long-time dean at the University of Georgia who passed on this week at age seventy-seven. He was one of the landmarks at the university, people used to say, and it was true. There were great reasons to admire the man. This is about just one. But first we need to think back to a different time, almost two decades ago, to 1961 when the University of Georgia admitted its first black students under a federal court order.

That is not so many years ago, really. Yet it is difficult to describe the tense emotional climate of that time in relation to school integration. There were brave men and women then, willing to stand up for fairness and equality at considerable personal risk. People lost jobs for daring to voice the notion that it was better to integrate the public schools than close the schools down.

There were also, apparently, otherwise decent men and women who fought hard to preserve racism as our sacred Southern way of life. In some ways, to borrow Charles Dickens's phrase, "It was the best of times and it was the worst of times." It is hard to convey the emotional intensity of those times in relation to something like the integration of the University of Georgia.

Well, then, the university did integrate. The first two black students admitted were Charlayne Hunter and Hamilton Holmes. Both, incidentally, finished at the university and went on to distinguished careers, Ms. Hunter as a journalist, currently a regular commentator on the "McNeil-Lehrer Report" on public television, Holmes to Emory Medical School and success as a physician.

A riot erupted within days, a huge bottle-throwing riot in front of the dormitory where Charlayne Hunter lived. Some of the sweet, young white coeds in the dormitory did their own little demonstration outside Charlayne's room. "Two, four, six, eight," some chanted, "we don't want to integrate." A shabby little exhibition. But why blame the coeds? This was a time when University of Georgia officials routinely went into federal courts and lied under oath to try to maintain segregation at the university. Why expect college students to do better than their elders? It was a time of sorry, puerile leadership in the state of Georgia.

University of Georgia officials to some extent let that riot happen, ignoring warnings from journalists telling them in advance what was planned that very evening. There were delays in calling for the State Patrol. Gov. Ernest Vandiver, who later exercised modern leadership in calling for peaceful school desegregation, felt caught that night by his own rhetoric, his campaign pledge to permit no integration while he was governor. But on that occasion, rather than exercising leadership, the governor ordered the two black students removed from the university for their "own safety." They were quickly ordered back, of course, by a federal judge.

That riot night was not a proud time for Georgia. Yet there was an exception. Dean Bill Tate, though nearly sixty years old, was out among the rioters like a one-man security squad. Charlayne Hunter was just another student as far as the dean was concerned, and she had a right to be there in her dormitory, and by God students had no business trying to scare her and throwing rocks and bottles. Tate stalked through that mob like an avenging prophet, ordering students to calm down, and taking up identification cards from the more violent ones; one husky student punched Tate in the jaw, the dean responded by knocking the young man down.

Tate that night stood up for the best in his university and in Georgia in rare fashion. Georgians did not have much to cheer about on that tumultuous evening of rioting at the university, but a good share of what honor and glory there were came from Bill Tate's decency and courage.

Remembering
Macon Editor
Joe Parham

December 29, 1980

Joe Parham was a professional journalist, a friend, and that makes this, in a real way, an insider kind of piece; move on if you don't care about reading such.

He was editor of the *Macon News* for just over thirty years, up until the night he died, a week ago last Saturday, in his sleep, at age sixty-one. That's a lot of time on this kind of turf and Parham used his time well.

He was a fine writer, a storyteller of rare good fun and joy in the telling. He cared about what he did, not a universal quality among newspaper folk or in any other profession. He happened to like Macon, enjoyed his local people and the community; but his greater community was the whole world and he enjoyed all of that too.

He could be serious enough on issues of any magnitude. Once, not long ago, he was one of the editors asked to quiz President Jimmy Carter at a meeting of the American Association of Newspaper Editors. Joe was under a little pressure, in a sense, a Georgia editor putting the questions to a president of the United States who happened to be from Georgia. He was

at ease and relaxed, as he usually seemed to be, and his questions were serious and good.

His sense of humor could drive you slightly up the wall if,
that is, you happened to be trying more or less to control it. We
occasionally did a TV show, Joe and I, "Atlanta Week in Review" on channel eight, usually when the Georgia Press Association was meeting in Athens at the Center for Continuing
Education (where the public broadcasting TV station also has
its base). He was relaxed in that kind of circumstance, too.
That blasted Parham and Bo McLeod of Donalsonville newspaper fame were with me at the same time on one such show;
any alleged TV host foolish enough to put those two together
at the same time is not smart enough to be on TV.

We were talking, not too long after Jimmy Carter had been
elected president, about how the very first Southern president
in more than a century could possibly have made it to the
White House. Well, the talk was serious for a while, but then
Joe decided to try a new tack. The whole secret really was
grits, he explained. Southern folks eat grits from a very young
age and, though they allowed it was a little-known fact, grits
had certain special properties that affected the brain cells and
the glands and all sorts of other vital functions. Bo McLeod,
not one to let foolishness run on without taking part, chimed
in and for about five minutes or so he and Parham offered just
about the damnedest series of theories about the powers of
grits in relation to the South and the body that anyone in the
universe may ever have heard.

Joe Parham was just good fun. It was coincidental, no
doubt, but you sometimes wonder if God's hand is not in these
things. Joe had by chance written a column for Sunday a week
ago about his career as a journalist. The column was published the day after he died.

"It has been a long and happy life," he wrote, "So far, nothing humdrum about it. Something new every day—as fresh as
the events which happened over town, the state, the country
and the world."

He loved all those events, town or state or world. He loved
musing about them, writing about them, carrying wife Hazel

off to those spots where his journalistic colleagues gathered and telling the stories that came to him with the flair of a master.

We'll miss him.

Clarence Bacote
Taught and Made
Atlanta History

April 10, 1981

Dr. Clarence A. Bacote was being honored at something or other one evening and joked good-humoredly about now being retired.

There are three sure signs of getting old, Bacote told his audience. First, your memory starts to slip, he said. And then, he went on, with perfect timing and a pause, well, I can't remember the other two things. His audience laughed in appreciation, and no one enjoyed his joke more than Bacote himself.

Yet, Bacote, to give the line a serious turn, has not forgotten much over the years. Or to put it another way: he has perhaps forgotten more about Georgia history and Atlanta politics than most of us ever knew.

Bacote has made his share of history, too. He came south from Kansas City in 1930 and spent the next forty-seven years as professor of history at Atlanta University and Morehouse College.

He remembered later that his first night was a little like a baptism of fire; the Ku Klux Klan was marching through black neighborhoods. A Negro boy had been killed by some white youths, tensions were high, and the Klan wanted to demonstrate a little show of force.

Nor was that, of course, the only side of a segregated South when Clarence Bacote came to Atlanta. There were no black officers on the city's police force, and Bacote found himself "shocked" at the way black citizens were treated in local courts.

Bacote likes to tell the story about the late Mayor William Hartsfield's meeting with black leaders in the early 1940s to talk about improving city services for black citizens. "If you had 10,000 votes, we might be able to talk," Hartsfield said. Bacote does not remember Hartsfield as a racist even in those early days, but politicians just did not pay much attention to people who did not vote. Times changed with the registration of black voters. Bacote can remember the city election in 1949 when Hartsfield was seeking reelection and had just named the first eight Negro police officers in Atlanta. "We had a big rally at the Big Bethel AME Church," said Bacote later, and just as Hartsfield was about to speak, he had some of those first uniformed black police officers walk into the church.

Bacote served as chairman of the All-Citizens Registration Committee from 1949 to 1961, a group that tried not only to get black people to register to vote but also to vote together. This was sometimes condemned as the "bloc vote." Bacote remembers it with good cheer and without regret. "It was a weapon. I would have been glad if we hadn't had to bloc vote. But where would we be if we hadn't?" he once said.

Bacote has been a great teacher in ways that go far beyond his university duties. For years now, he has analyzed the voting trends in Atlanta by taking key precincts and sifting the results. He has also done a lot to keep journalists straight on matters of history. The first black state legislators in a long, long while were elected in Georgia in the mid-1960s. A lot of us tended to think that there had been black elected officials in the South for a brief time during Reconstruction, after the Civil War, and then an all-white cast in Southern legislatures for the next hundred years. Not really so. The Jim Crow segregation patterns were clamped down slowly over a period of three decades or more. McIntosh County elected a black Republican to the Georgia House as late as 1904 and 1906.

It all comes to mind in part because Clarence Bacote was honored the other day with a special gold medallion by the State Committee on the Life and History of Black Georgians. He deserves such honors. He has honored his chosen city, Atlanta, both by teaching its history and by helping shape that history for the better.

Roasting
Bob Steed
in Macon

May 5, 1981

A bunch of us went from Atlanta down to Macon last Friday by chartered bus and cars and maybe even pogo sticks in order to attend a roast of one Robert L. Steed.

Lord knows why, exactly. Perhaps a spirit of compassion. Steed, of course, is the failed bond lawyer who occasionally writes an allegedly humorous column for this newspaper. It is likely that so many people turned up at the dinner-roast for fear that nobody would be there at all.

It was a wondrous occasion in its way, held at the Macon city auditorium. Some said it was the most unusual event held in that building since the Georgia Democratic party met there in 1966 to nominate Lester Maddox for governor. The Steed roast indeed had something in common with that 1966 Democratic party session; there were a lot of people wandering around with glazed eyes saying to each other, "Why am I here?"

Former Macon Mayor Buck Melton presided at the roast. Melton is known as The Old Mayor. That is because he is no longer mayor now and because he married a pretty woman roughly forty-six years younger than he is. He is thinking about running for governor next year and his wife may let him just to get him out of the house. Macon Mayor George Israel is currently in office and he is known as The Young Mayor. That is because he has a pretty wife and two young children, the youngest a baby several months old. Israel may run for governor next year to get out of the house and not have to change diapers.

Steed was in pretty fair form for a bond lawyer, which means that in his remarks he was able to put several declarative sentences together in sequence, each with a verb and a subject. In some cases the verb and subject were in the same tense. His friends and colleagues tried to help him all they could.

Several people wanted to know why the *Atlanta Constitution* ran Steed's columns on any basis, since they clearly damaged the reputations of lawyers and journalists alike. There is something in that, but only if you accept the premise that lawyers and journalists have enough reputations left to damage.

The state of Georgia used to hire lawyers to preserve segregation and the old Southern ways, and we called them great constitutional lawyers; that meant that the state could pay them a lot of money to lose cases all the way up to the U. S. Supreme Court. Steed is in the bond-lawyer field, the equivalent of a great constitutional lawyer.

It is in this context that some of us have puzzled over why Steed even wants to write columns, why this dubious drive to embarrass himself in two fields at once? The reason came to me quite accidentally. On Saturday, the day after the Steed roast in Macon, the Ansley Park Civic Association had its annual Spring Fling, which means hot dogs and beer and music and outdoor things. The music was good, Bluegrass variety, and it turned out the fellow leading the picking and singing was Mike Steed, younger brother of Robert Steed. Now, Mike somewhat resembles brother Bob, but he is young enough so that the doctors say there is every hope he will grow out of that. The younger Steed lives in Bowdon and during the week poses as a manufacturing representative, but what he really does is sing and play music and very well, too. It suddenly struck me: Robert Steed seems so driven because he discovered at some early stage of life that there was actually talent in the family, if in a sibling, and he has been trying to overcompensate ever since.

Mercer University Press, in what seems quite an overreaction to Bob Steed's supposed contributions to his alma mater, has just published a volume—*Willard Lives!*—of Steed's columns from his student newspaper days and other columns written for the Younger Lawyers Section Newsletter. As Steed himself observes, this establishes again the relevance of those two old verities: 1. Nobody ever went broke by underestimating the taste of the American public. 2. The evil that men do lives after them, while the good is often interred with their bones.

On the Death of Our Friend, Omar Torrijos

August 4, 1981

General Omar Torrijos, as good a friend as the United States had in this hemisphere, will be buried today after lying in state for twenty-four hours so that his mourning Panamanian countrymen could pay their last respects.

They took his body Monday up to the top of Ancon Hill, overlooking the Panama Canal, for a memorial ceremony. That was a fitting tribute. Torrijos and former President Jimmy Carter hammered out the treaties in 1977 and 1978 that will turn the Panama Canal over to Panama by the end of the century. Torrijos and Carter both understood, as perhaps some Americans did not at the time, that the existing Panama Canal agreement was viewed as a poisonous remnant of colonial power throughout the rest of the world. The success of the newly negotiated treaty for the United States is the spiritual triumph of the most powerful nation in the world showing fairness and dignity to a far smaller nation, not because Panama could force us to do so, but because it was right and just that we do so. Torrijos raised a Panamanian flag out on the top of Ancon Hill when the treaties were approved.

He was killed Friday in a light plane crash in the mountains west of Panama City, on his way to the small village of Coclecito. I flew over those same mountains once with Torrijos, on a happier day with better weather, when we made it safely to Coclecito. It is a small village, of no more perhaps than 300 people. Torrijos had a house there, nothing fancy, and he had rather adopted the little town—helping the people there improve farming methods and water supply. His friends said he liked to get away to the little village a day or two each week to "keep his feet on the ground."

I visited with Torrijos in Coclecito only days before the U. S. Senate was to vote, up or down, on the approval of the negotiated treaties. He was typically called the Panamanian "strong man" who had taken over the government in 1968 and, with the support of the National Guard, had at that point been running Panama for a decade.

Yet with all his occasional flamboyance—typically the cigar with a General Omar Torrijos band on it and the army fatigues and the pistol on one hip—he seemed almost philosophical about holding on to power. He had patiently met with delegation after delegation of U. S. senators, to the point that he felt at times, as he put it, "as if I am on trial before 100 senators." He thought the Panama Canal treaties were terribly important, both for his country and the United States, to the point that he was willing to say that he would give up power, step aside as the "strong man" of his government, if that were necessary to win approval of the treaties.

He liked Americans. He had an almost naive trust that in the end most Americans wanted to do the right thing, that for this reason alone the treaties would surely be approved.

God knows why, in a way. We gave Omar Torrijos enough reason to dislike us over the years. He was nine or ten years old when his mother once took him through the Panama Canal Zone, on the way to Panama City to shop for clothes for school. An American policeman from the Zone boarded the bus, pulled his mother aside roughly, and began searching her packages. A small incident maybe. Torrijos remembered it vividly all his life, how his mother had been pushed around and treated rudely.

He seized power in Panama in 1968, supported by other younger army officers who were convinced that their government was corrupt. Torrijos, whose parents were both school-teachers, was especially outraged that the government would allot money for schools and then the politicians would manage to steal most of it before it got transferred to the educational system. His perhaps proudest boast was that after ten years in power, there were some 30,000 public schoolteachers in his country; there were only 8,000 teachers when he assumed power.

We gave the general another reason to be fond of the United States after he had been in power about one year. Our ace intelligence operatives out of the Canal Zone encouraged several army officers to overthrow Torrijos in 1969, while he was on a visit to Mexico City. He didn't care much for that, nor did it intimidate him. He flew back to Panama and to the Army barracks at the town of David; the troops there professed loyalty. Torrijos started marching with these troops from David to Panama City, picking up thousands of people in the towns along the way. By the time the crowds were greeting him at the outskirts of Panama City, the officers trying to overthrow Torrijos were trying to figure out how to get out of the country.

Despite that memory of the incident with his mother, of our attempt to overthrow him, and of the phony charge by some U. S. senators that Torrijos was involved in the narcotics trade, he continued to like and admire Americans and was both delighted and moved when the Panama Canal treaties were finally approved by the Senate.

Torrijos offered to let the shah of Iran seek sanctuary in Panama when it seemed that might be of help in winning freedom for the American hostages in Iran. Hamilton Jordan flew down to ask for his help, and Torrijos agreed at once, knowing full well that there would probably be some demonstrations in his country in protest against the shah.

Omar Torrijos was the strong man of Panama all right, a military dictator, if you will, but a man far more complete and decent than those phrases suggest. He was a man who loved his country and who hated injustice, a man whose heart was with the peasants and the poor of his country, for he wanted them to have opportunities that their parents and grandparents never had. He tried to explain his feelings about those things to me once, how his parents had been schoolteachers and poor, devoutly religious without any drive for money. "I can live," he said, "without the comfort of a bed. I can go to bed alone or without pajamas. But you cannot go to bed without a conscience."

Anwar Sadat
Had the Courage
to Make Peace

October 7, 1981

Anwar Sadat was one of the great men of history, one of the rare ones who in part shape their times, in this case for the better.

Those who hold that all of history is shaped totally by mechanical or social forces of some order are idiots, whatever their academic credentials. They fail to trust their own hearts, their own individual capacities. Sure there are, no doubt, forces moving sometimes with historic implications, with the odds against any individual stopping or changing them utterly. But there are the compelling instances, too, of individuals who made a huge difference in the world as it existed. There are the Hitlers and those who create evil. There are the rare ones, a Sadat, who found the strength and courage to make peace in a troubled part of the world, which had not known peace in his lifetime.

Sadat was a most interesting man, all else aside. He was one of the group of soldiers, along with Gamal Abdel Nasser, who overthrew the British and removed a king. Yet somewhere along the way, he picked up a concern for his people that went beyond any simple desire for political power.

It is sometimes so easy to misread individuals. Sadat was rather intensely loyal to Nasser, even when he saw that Nasser was making mistakes. He simply did not seem to possess that fierce personal ambition visible in Nasser and others jockeying for power in Egypt and in the Middle East. His apparent lack of ambition made him more trusted by those who thirsted for power. Nasser made him second in power, in title at least, in government. At Nasser's death, however, the general belief was that Sadat was a weak man, a fellow who would serve as an interim figurehead while the real jockeying for control of the government continued. Nothing could have been further from the truth, as events and history demonstrated.

Sadat's strengths were deeply set and of a philosophical, almost mystical base. In his autobiography, *In Search of Identity*, Sadat began: "I, Anwar el-Sadat, a peasant born and brought up on the banks of the Nile—where man first witnessed the dawn of time—present this book to readers everywhere." He had a sense of history and believed in a real way that the events of his own life coincided with the important events of Egypt during his lifetime. He never grew completely away from that little village where he grew up, Mit Abul-Kum; and as president of Egypt he still contributed his personal moneys to a fund set up to make this or that kind of improvement in village living conditions.

He was imprisoned a couple of times by the British during World War II and he came later to remember his months in cell 54 at Cairo Central Prison as a period of great personal growth.

"Inside Cell 54," he wrote in his autobiography, "as my material needs grew increasingly less, the ties which had bound me to the material world began to be severed, one after another. . . . So long as a man is enslaved by material needs—wanting to be or to possess one thing or another—nothing will ever belong to him; he will always belong to 'things.' A slave to things does not exist as a human being; only when he has ceased to need things, can a man truly be his own master and so really exist."

I met Sadat once, at Jimmy Carter's home in Plains when the Egyptian president paid a visit in August. I told him I thought I understood him better after reading about his experiences in cell 54. He was good enough to autograph my copy of his book. I will value that, a memento of a great man, an individual who made a difference in history and for the better.

On Naming
a City Street
after Abby

May 17, 1982

The city of Atlanta renamed a street the other day. A stretch of Sixth Street has now become Abercrombie Place.

The "Abercrombie" of the name was present at the ceremonies, delighted that Mayor Andrew Young and other officials and friends had turned out in numbers to wish him well. It is fairly rare, if not completely unknown, to name any street after someone still alive, and Abercrombie is not only alive and well, he is also still full of energy and verve. He was tickled the other day at all the hoopla.

His full name is E. L. Abercrombie. He is known well by the waitresses at the Commerce Club, which fills up at lunchtime on most days with a remarkably establishment-looking business crowd. Mr. Abercrombie appears to fit in well enough, in conservative dark suit and with rather distinguished white hair.

It is more likely than not, though, that on any given day he may be the only union leader in the room. He is called Mr. Abercrombie at the Commerce Club. He has been called some rather more harsh names by people who crossed him either in a labor or a political fight. He is called Abby by his friends.

The offices of his union, the Laundry, Dry Cleaning, and Dye House Workers, Local 218, are at the corner of Spring Street and the street now named Abercrombie Place. That's been Abby's union for more than thirty-five years and, as executive secretary-treasurer, he's run it effectively in the interest of members in fourteen states. At age seventy-four, he has allegedly retired, but nobody who knows him believes it. He remains secretary emeritus of the union and stays active also in the international part of the union, headquartered in Chicago.

Abby's reputation as an effective union leader rests in some curious combination of feisty common sense, persistence, honesty, and a compelling intensity when dealing with the needs of his people. People tend to trust him, even when butting heads in battle. No one seems to doubt that he'll get done anything he promises to get done, that a handshake on an agreement is as binding as any contract. His fiercest criticisms, in conversation, are of people who promise him to do something a certain way and then fail to carry out the agreement.

To some extent Abby's labor connections in Atlanta span forty years of the city's history. He dropped out of school after the sixth grade, and by the early 1930s he was driving a taxi in Atlanta. That was his first labor battle. A fellow named Al Belle Isle had close to a monopoly on taxis in the city. The story told was that Abby took him on and "broke Belle Isle." He tells it more modestly. "I didn't break Belle Isle," he told Margaret Shannon in one interview. "We just put automobiles on the street and hauled people free. That was an easy strike. He came around fast."

There perhaps have been tough times in his career. Early in his laundry-union days, there were separate white and black unions. The white workers didn't make much, $18 per week at the time. The black workers made only a fraction of that. Abby moved to combine the two unions and led them in a strike for better wages; the strike lasted twelve months and five days.

One of his more recent battles involved taking on the Atlanta Housing Authority on any number of issues, after those employed by the authority came to him and asked that Abby's union represent them.

There have, no doubt, been some frightening times, too. There was a time when some gangster elements made a serious effort to take over the laundry workers' union. Abby went to Fulton County District Attorney Lewis Slaton after a death threat. Slaton looked into the matter, decided it was a serious threat, and for a time kept undercover law officers on a protective watch.

Abercrombie Place. It has a nice, solid, dignified ring to it. But how do you ask a fellow to lunch who already has a street named after him?

Part IV

Personal Biases
and Other
Good Fun

Some essays in this section are serious, many are not. Some of the merely semiserious topics include whether Sir James Oglethorpe, founder of Georgia, might not have been on the right track when he wanted the original colonists to bar lawyers and strong drink, and whether or not you have to be an IRSOB to work for the IRS. Others involve some wondrous belly dancers in Cairo, within sight of the pyramids, and the dastardly effort (as the college administrators saw it) of *Playboy* magazine to seduce Baylor coeds, and even Julian Bond's notorious "Seal Boy Hoax."

More serious efforts include an essay from the Sea of Galilee and a piece on the traumatic ordeal of the kidnapping in 1974 of Reg Murphy, then editor of the *Atlanta Constitution*.

Gray Grimness
Makes Us
Grateful

June 9, 1969

There *are* those days when you become almost pathetically grateful for small things. You know, when you have worries of your own, more or less, and when with the best will in the world you just don't *care* what President Nixon reportedly told several congressmen privately last Thursday. Or, whether or not the Georgia legislature comes back to town (ever). Or, say, whether Art lives in Atlanta (anymore). Or, if it's *really* true that you can't trust anyone under thirty.

And, when you happen to recall Spiro T. Agnew's latest comment about something, and it fails to make you *smile* . . . that is a certain sign of the Gray Grimness.

Ah, well it is then that the small news items are enough to give one strength and heart (and you know, you've *got* to have heart). For instance, it's fascinating to read that Christine Keeler, the playgirl who cost a British cabinet minister his government post in 1963, turned up the other day at a press reception for American movie star Steve McQueen. Asked what she'd been doing since dropping from public view, Miss Keeler replied: "I just sort of mess around in general."

Then, there was the little story out of Hartshorne, Oklahoma, about a class being held for young ladies who want to learn how to shoot a bow and arrow. The class is taught by palefaces, members of the Little Dixie Bowmen Club, at the Jones Academy gymnasium.

Of course, there is the startling news that the North Carolina House has approved a bill to make the gray squirrel the official state mammal. During the debate on the matter, one legislator rose to declare, "I would like to say that an animal that can bury nuts could be dangerous to this General Assembly."

Also, it was comforting to know that at least one judge in the Atlanta area is willing to put a young man in jail for sixty days on a minor traffic violation unless the twenty-one-year-old salesman agreed to cut off his shoulder-length long hair. Certainly seemed a mighty stroke for law and order and against crime in the street and so forth.

Good, too, that any number of other long-haired gentlemen didn't face this kind of justice in our enlightened era. Imagine Jesus Christ, Richard the Lion-Hearted, or Thomas Jefferson facing a choice like that. A short haircut, sir, or sixty days.

Oh, one other small thing, though hardly a news item. I said to a small boy, aged six and a half: "What should I write a column about?" Quoth he, thoughtfully: "Why don't you write about my new bicycle?"

The bicycle in question has a red seat, high handlebars, and is altogether a handsome artifact. Its young rider does quite well going down hills, but has some difficulty coming back up and on turns. But he is improving, thank you.

Sometimes,
You Can Fight
City Hall

July 11, 1969

LOUISVILLE GA—Maybe you can't fight city hall. Maybe you shouldn't even try. How can you win? Maybe one individual can't take on the U. S. Navy.

Rhodes Hardeman, a stocky, soft-spoken businessman, has been running Hardeman Seed Co. here for some years. He's a member of the Kiwanis Club, interested in civic things, but you get the impression he stays pretty busy most of the time. Not a man, particularly, to seek out lost causes, or to stir up trouble for anyone.

He's not really wildly enthusiastic about finding himself in the position of being critical of the Navy. "A newspaper is different, like the *Constitution* or the *Journal*. It's a big organization. I'm just one man," says Hardeman, then adding good-humoredly (but with some seriousness), "You know, the Navy is liable to have the FBI down here investigating me."

It was Hardeman who first raised public questions about the Navy's handling of the body of a Navy enlisted man from Louisville, Chief Petty Officer Robert Middleton. After Middleton's death in May, the Navy shipped the body home for burial in Louisville where he'd grown up and where his parents, Mr. and Mrs. Henry Middleton, still live.

The widow came to Louisville for the burial, but then later changed her mind and asked Navy officials to help her have the body taken from Louisville and reburied in the national cemetery at Andersonville, Georgia. The Navy made the necessary arrangements with an Augusta funeral vault company, including obtaining for the company the appropriate authorization from the widow as immediate next of kin.

Only one problem. Nobody let the parents know. The first word the parents received was the information that two men from Augusta were digging up their son's grave. Before anyone could take action . . . even find out what was happening . . . it was all over . . . the grave opened up . . . the body gone. The parents, at that point, had no idea even where their son's body was being taken.

Henry Middleton has worked for Hardeman Seed Co. for years, which is how Rhodes Hardeman got involved. "Henry is a good man. He's reliable. He's honest . . . I just hated to see anybody get pushed around . . . taken advantage of," says Hardeman. "When I called Port Hueneme [the California base where Middleton was stationed], I wasn't trying to put anybody on the spot . . . all we wanted to know is where . . . [he] was buried," Hardeman recalls.

Navy officials at the base said they didn't know exactly what had happened, but promised to find out and let Hardeman know. After almost a full week, with no reply or information, Hardeman contacted the *Atlanta Constitution*.

There is a kind of Southern paternalistic note in this, maybe. Rhodes Hardeman is a successful white businessman. Henry Middleton is a relatively uneducated laboring black man, left bewildered and hurt by what has happened. Hardeman clearly feels a responsibility. "Henry has always been a damned good man with me. He has the keys to my business. He could come in here," gesturing at his office, "in the middle of the night if he wanted," Hardeman says. "I just didn't want anybody walking on him. . . ."

For more than three weeks, the U. S. Navy refused to offer any explanation to the Louisville parents, insisting that Navy regulations did not *require* it. Secretary of the Navy John Chaffee took a more compassionate view this week, with a letter to the Middleton parents, explaining what had happened and expressing "my personal regrets that you have suffered additional grief in the loss of your son."

"That's all anybody ever wanted," said Hardeman, "just that they do something decent." Maybe sometimes you fight city hall . . . and win.

Sea of Galilee: A Peaceful Place

December 2, 1972

SEA OF GALILEE—It is all within Israel now, this inland fresh-water sea whose very name conjures up echoes of the beginnings of Christianity.

That was not true up until the Six-Day War five years ago. The extreme north end was, in effect, controlled by Syria. The borders of Syria, Jordan, and Israel all touch near here. The cease-fire lines of 1967 pushed the borders of Syria and Jordan back a bit. It's not so easy now for Syrian cannons to drop shells into Israeli settlements, though it still happens.

The Golan Heights rise in brown and sand-colored cliffs near this Sea of Galilee. Seen from a boat, those cliffs seem partly to surround this six-by-twelve-mile sea like the edge of a saucer. It was from those cliffs and hills that the Syrian soldiers used to fire their cannons. It is the reason why the Israelis are unlikely in any peace settlements to give up the Golan Heights. They remember those cannon and mortar shells.

There is a restaurant called Ein-Gev at one side of the water, the side nearest Jordan, owned by a nearby kibbutzim community. It is pleasant and tasteful with clay-colored walls and outdoor tables. They will serve you a delicious fried fish, called "St. Peter's fish" because it is caught in the Sea of Galilee, where Peter was a fisherman until Jesus recruited him to be a fisher of men.

"Jesus was walking by the Sea of Galilee," as Matthew told it, "when he saw two brothers, Simon called Peter and his brother Andrew, casting a net into the lake; for they were fishermen. Jesus said to them, 'Come with me, and I will make you fishers of men.' And at once they left their nets and followed him."

It is a sunny day and the sea seems placid and quiet. There are fish literally jumping out of the water, and a man who knows says there is still very good fishing here. Several kinds of fish for the catching in addition to the St. Peter's fish.

From the dock near the Ein-Gev restaurant, you can take a boat across the sea to Tiberias, a village that has been on the bank of the Sea of Galilee since the time when Jesus walked there. It is an old sort of resort town. There are sulphur springs and long ago people came for their health. Capernaum is nearby, the little town where Matthew says Jesus moved when he left Nazareth. There is a sign at Capernaum. "The Town of Jesus," it says. An admission ticket costs about ten cents. Many of the stories of the four Gospels about Jesus involve this inland Sea of Galilee.

It was on these shores that he recruited not only Simon (called Peter) and his brother Andrew but two other brothers, James and John, both sons of Zebedee. Tradition has it that his most famous sermon, the Sermon on the Mount, was delivered near this sea, on a gently rising hill now called the Mount of Beatitudes. There is a monastery at the top of the hill today.

It was here too, on these shores, that Jesus blessed the five loaves and two fishes and fed a great crowd of more than 5,000 and where he walked across the water to a boat being rowed against a heavy head wind by several of his disciples who, Mark relates, were terrified until he told them, "Take heart! It is I; do not be afraid." Mark goes on, "Then he climbed into the boat besides them, and the wind dropped. At this they were completely dumbfounded, for they had not understood the incident of the loaves; their minds were closed."

In Jerusalem, at some of the traditional, most sacred places of Christianity, the hawkers of cheap tinsel and shoddy souvenirs are in abundance. The churchmen aren't much better, pushing for money in a fashion reminiscent of the cheap salesmen-types Jesus once ran out of the Temple. The Sea of Galilee and the hills around it refresh the spirit. They are beautiful. They don't seem to have changed much in 2,000 years.

The News
with Love
from Spring Street

June 7, 1973

The "Spring's News and Views" is, to paraphrase Daniel Webster from quite another context, a small newspaper, but there are those who love it.

It is a publication of limited budget and circulation, but with the great asset of considerable young talent and the help and advice of one somewhat older (if not grayer) head. It has a certain style, made up of equal parts enthusiasm, competence, variety of interests, and innocence.

The large headlines on page one, "The Fifth Grade Flash" and underneath "Vacation Begins," are perhaps a bit showy, akin to the "Spring Is Here" of an earlier edition. But they are certainly effective and to the point.

The weather report in the upper left-hand corner of last Tuesday's third (and final) edition of the year reads "Hot, Temp, High 89," which turned out to be pretty accurate; but it then reads "Fair Cumulus Clouds," a prediction that, alas, went awry and awash in that afternoon and evening's late thunderstorms.

The masthead of this limited-edition, fifteen-page issue includes science and music and literary editors, not to mention sports and joke and food editors, along with just editor-editors and even an Around the World editor.

There is a certain historical touch in the form of a distinguished essay on Patrick Henry by a Ms. Margaret Cook, written from the point of view of Patrick Henry's guardian angel. And there is a hint of the topical energy-crisis concern in the editor's note warning not to drive too fast on the roads this summer because, "You use less gas."

There is also an apparent immediate concern about the Watergate mess with no fewer than four separate articles by varying staff members, each with definite viewpoints. "Most people have faith in the country, but not the people who have been picked for our government," wrote one Kevin Cleveland, who holds that enviable title of Around the World editor. "The President should have paid more attention," continues Cleveland. "He made a speech totaling about 4,000 words," he goes on, and then with a rhetorical flourish: "What is Watergate going to do to Nixon? If Nixon has been caught in this mess impeachment will become of Nixon."

Cleveland has other interesting comments: "Kathern Gram's paper brought out most of the Watergate [story]. . . . After this mess is cleared up the nation will be the same. No matter how many new laws there are we will always be free and have the right to vote. We will be the same. It does not matter how many people are in jail the country will never depart. . . . Our Government has saved and struggled out harder things than the Watergate Follies. For example: World War I and World War II and Vietnam."

One young lady, Ms. Tish Hamilton, has a more direct and personal point of view: "Let's talk about Watergate. It's impossible not to know about Watergate these days, but humans have different opinions. My opinion is that Nixon is guilty. I think that he is not doing it all though . . . I think the Watergate Affair is ridiculous! But it is interesting to find out about it. I even bet that, as a kid, the Watergate 'Bad' guys, were

School 'Bad' guys. It seems that this country will always have a bit of mischief!!"

Away from politics, my favorite articles include one about Sweden, one about middle schools ("I personally think it is a great idea, because it would be better to have a school with age groups closer together than to have a school with age groups far apart like Elementary schools and regular high schools have") and one called, with a splendid title, "Throwing Things Should Not Be Done." These three are by a talented ten-year-old who signs himself Harold Gulliver.

Finally, it is nice to read the closing note from Mrs. Frances Elyea (that older if not grayer head) who retires as a schoolteacher this year and wrote to her newspaper staff, "Please remember what I have taught you about good attitudes, kindness, respect for others and honesty. . . . Love to every one of you."

Reg Murphy's 49-hour Ordeal (and Ours)

February 28, 1974

Nightmares move quickly on occasion, though they seem long enough at the time. It was just one week ago today editor Reg Murphy was in the first grim hours of his kidnapping ordeal, and in that first, tense stage his friends and colleagues at this newspaper had literally no idea if he was alive or dead.

The first telephone calls the night before had announced that he was being held by the "American revolutionary army." One of the fearful things in that first period of hours was that no one knew really what that meant. No one knew what particular brand of crazies had taken Murphy from his home, nor what in the world the demands might turn out to be. Money? Maybe, but no one knew for certain. Feed the poor? Or some specific political demand? No one knew.

Murphy himself obviously was in the process of enduring incredible tension and pressure at that time. But there was tension enough at the newspaper, compounded by the near-total frustration of knowing that there really wasn't much of anything to be done until the kidnappers made renewed contact, made their demands.

Oh, there were some things done, the things that could be done. The Federal Bureau of Investigation moved into the case at once with a sure skill that earned the deepest admiration from everyone who had contact with the FBI during the harrowing forty-nine-hour ordeal. Impressive too was the careful insistence of the FBI that they wanted to do nothing at any stage that could endanger Murphy's life, and that the critical decisions to be made rested first with Murphy's family and then with the newspaper.

It was a time of heightened awareness in some ways, and there are a lot of small scenes and impressions that remain. A vivid one. Jack Tarver, president of the Atlanta newspapers, first getting the news that the kidnappers had made contact and wanted $700,000.

He reached instantly for the telephone to call the Federal Reserve Bank and find out how long it would take them to get $700,000 ready, and then hesitated, realizing that the kidnappers would probably specify later that they wanted the money in certain numbers of $50s or $100s or whatever (as they subsequently did).

Or Tarver plowing like an irritated bull through a group of television cameras in front of Murphy's house after one television newsman had asked one foolish question too many. Tarver had wanted to go by the house himself to assure Murphy's family that everything that could be done was being done. And while it probably wasn't good public relations to push your way through a circle of news folk, the people who had watched Tarver bear the main responsibility of what amounted to life-and-death decision making with grace and guts took a certain perverse, good-humored satisfaction in seeing the Tarver charge on some TV news accounts.

There were so many people who did well. The Cox family, owners of this newspaper, were supportive throughout. Jim Kennedy, grandson of the late Gov. James Cox, was on hand at the newspaper during most of the tense times. One memory that stays is of Kennedy and Jeff Nesmith hurriedly drawing maps of the North Fulton County area where the $700,000 ransom, crammed into two suitcases, was to be dropped by

Managing Editor Jim Minter. Minter, who can properly be considered a genuine hero for his courageous role in a difficult
time, was terribly afraid of one thing: the North Fulton area
where he was to follow directions and leave the money is a good
distance from his own home, an area he didn't know at all; and
he was fearful of having trouble finding the exact spot when
Murphy's life might depend on the money being delivered at a
certain time. Minter took the maps along, to be sure he
wouldn't take a wrong turn.

Ah, well, there were curiously some funny things too. In a
situation so grim, either you laugh from time to time, or you
cry. Joe Brown, editorial associate, was out of the city when
the kidnapping occurred and flew back in at once. "I go out of
town for a few days," he grumbled at one point, "and you lose
Murphy."

Should Lawyers Still Be Barred from Georgia?

June 9, 1975

SAVANNAH GA—A character created by William Shake-speare, one in the second part of *Henry VI*, once commented, no doubt in the vein of an early social reformer, "The first thing we do, let's kill all the lawyers."

If someone had dropped a bomb of moderate size on down-town Savannah last Thursday or Friday, it would have gone a long way towards doing in a goodly part of the lawyers and judges in Georgia as members of the State Bar gathered in all their glory for their annual meeting.

There is some irony in the State Bar's preference for Savannah in which to hold such gatherings. My colleague Joe Brown assures me that Georgia's founding and guiding spirit, Sir James Oglethorpe, had only two rules when he brought the first colonists to Georgia and with Colonel Bull laid out the streets and squares of Savannah. Oglethorpe's rules: no rum and no lawyers. It is hard to imagine what Oglethorpe might have made of a modern State Bar meeting.

A careful effort to verify colleague Brown's report had mixed results. Oglethorpe helped select the original Georgia colonists and he wanted people of strong character not given to strong drink, so maybe that part rings right. On barring lawyers? Well, that was harder to research. There apparently weren't many lawyers around in any case. A book on Georgia history by Amanda Johnson reports that in the early days justice was administered mostly by the town court in Savannah, which had three bailiffs and a recorder. The court dealt with matters such as treason, counterfeiting, insurrection, trespass, debt, and also "ordinary crimes," such as, according to Ms. Johnson, "when a soldier offered to sell his wife and another offered to buy her, this constituting a misdemeanor."

There weren't many lawyers though, seemingly, since each defendant pleaded his own case. "It was hopeless to try to secure justice," says Ms. Johnson, "for although the common law of England was used, those who administered it were frequently ignorant of the law and quarrelsome men. No law books existed in the colony until 1741, and it mattered little, for some of the judges could neither read nor write."

There are some who would say that the situation has not absolutely, utterly, changed since 1741. I certainly would not say that myself, however.

Ah, well. Enough, enough. It is not entirely safe to jest about lawyers, as Harold Clarke is my witness. I mentioned Clarke, an old friend (there, that'll embarrass him), in a column the other day observing that the former legislator was alive and well in Forsyth, where he was practicing law and probably engaging in other equally dubious pursuits. One lawyer wrote State Bar President Stell Huie demanding that the leaders of the bar take action to stop such terrible attacks. Clarke, who was just made president-elect of the State Bar, was in my view overly sympathetic to this approach. He told me that he wasn't completely sure what the best way to stop a columnist might be but that, after it was worked out, he certainly wanted to be included in the ceremonies.

In truth, lawyers even in great batches, as they were in Savannah last week, are as individuals probably the brightest, most interesting, varied, and creative professionals in our society.

Only 359 Days until the Next Great Race

July 10, 1977*

This year's Peachtree Road Race of July 4th turned out to be a great event, a happening of the first order.

At this point, six days after the race, most of the aching muscles have eased and the close to 100 runners who passed out with heat exhaustion have, one hopes, all recovered completely and are telling war stories about their adventures. That's one nice thing about the event, of course. There were rumors aplenty on the day of the race that one or two or more people had died on the spot, from coronary problems or whatever, during the 6.2-mile course; but apparently the fully 6,000 runners taking part all survived, a cheerful aspect of what turned out to be a thoroughly cheerful and good-humored event.

It was fun, plain and simple, even for the staggering semi-runners like me who tottered across the finish line downtown after a while. I admit to finishing behind Lasse Viren and

*This essay originally appeared in the Sunday *Atlanta Journal and Constitution*.

Frank Shorter and even Jim Kennedy and Lee May, but that is as much as I am willing to say about my exact finishing sequence. It is a lie, however, that I took a taxi in the middle stretch, a rumor spread by publisher Jack Tarver. I also deny that I crawled in on my hands and knees for the last three or four blocks.

Not only that, I was able to expose sports editor Jesse Outlar for the shallow, casual sports prophet that he is; he picked me to finish 6,000th in a field of 6,000, and I was certainly no further back than 5,659th. What does Outlar know?

I was touched by some expressions of concern from friendly districts before I ran in the great race. One nice lady, a former neighbor, wrote a sweet note and pointed out that it was a long way from Buckhead to downtown Atlanta, that it would be hot and humid, and what would I gain anyway? A T-shirt? She voiced worry that I might do myself harm. I appreciated her thought, and she was quite right in every detail.

It was a long way, and it was hot and humid, and I considered it quite possible that I was doing myself permanent harm after the first 1.8 miles when that bloody Peachtree Street starts going uphill at a terrible rate. It is a wonder to me that Sherman's troops ever made it.

I also appreciated the note from a gentleman who wanted to correct me on an error in which I apparently engaged as did some other journalists, referring to the Road Racers Club of America when the correct name is Road Runners Club of America. They are the national group that approved the Peachtree Road Race as its official 10,000-meter championship race. He added, in a friendly vein, that if I was serious about not being in top running form for the run, that he would "like to suggest (for your own personal health and safety) that you abandon plans to run in this grueling, hot race." I thought of his phrasing several times.

Whatever happened to Councilman Richard Guthman anyway? He alleges he finished in under the 55-minute time, the time necessary to win a T-shirt, but I never saw him. Some might say that was because I was so far behind; however, I may note that Guthman said in one of his threatening letters to me (those that kept reminding me that I had said I would run if he would run) that he would be there at the finish line to greet me. He wasn't there. In any case, if Guthman really got there in fifty-five minutes or less, it was probably by taking a MARTA bus.

Ah, well. It is a great event by any measure. And there is both a delightful and serious side to it too: anything that focuses that kind of attention on good exercise, on staying in something like reasonable physical shape and good health has got to be good for everyone who gets involved. Fun too.

Eddie Slovik's
Panic Was
Not His Alone

February 8, 1978

The sweet-tempered British poets of World War I were among the last to write romantically about war, the glory of the battlefield and the honor of getting your legs shot off for your country.

Ernest Hemingway had such impact on the generation following that war, in part because he wrote about slaughter with some perception that it included blood and pain and often terrible injustice. Maybe the good don't always die young, but it is generally young people who march into battle and give their lives, sometimes in a good cause, sometimes not.

It comes to mind because of the decision to give some consideration to the widow of Private Eddie Slovik, the only—get that now, literally the only—American serviceman to be executed for desertion in World War II. President Carter has asked the Congress to approve some $70,000 in back insurance payments for Antoinette Slovik, the widow, payments denied because her husband was executed. She currently is quite poor, confined to a wheelchair and dependent on welfare checks to survive. She has repeatedly asked the government to permit her to collect on her husband's insurance policy, a request the government has stoutly denied, not to its credit.

Carter's request comes at a time when there is considerable sentiment to right an old wrong. There recently was a television dramatization of the Slovik story. Leaders in Congress, Senate Democrat Robert Byrd is one, have urged Carter to support such a special action.

The history is melancholy. It was World War II and a hard time. It was visibly the last stage of the war. American troops had landed in Europe and were fighting to win at a time when it seemed clear that they would win. But the battles were bitter and fierce and there were, in some battles, desertions of troops in frightening numbers.

It was in this unhappy context that Private Eddie Slovik found himself. He deserted twice, running away in combat, torn with fear. Both times, he turned himself over to authorities and told them that his personal panic had overcome him in battle.

In another time a wise sergeant might have discreetly gotten Slovik transferred to the rear lines. In this particular time, Slovik was viewed as an example of the soldier deserting under fire, the kind of example that must be faced and disciplined. Charges were filed, the case put; he was found guilty of deserting under fire, and sentenced to death. It is probable (if not certain) that those passing sentence believed that they were setting the example, yet that some higher authority would surely overrule the death sentence.

The higher authorities reviewed the case. It went right up to the supreme commander of allied troops, one Dwight David Eisenhower. In another time the supreme commander might have commuted the sentence. But that was a time of high tension, of concern about desertions. Generals panic too. Ike did not have the perception or courage to commute that sentence; and it was so that a young, frightened soldier, Eddie Slovik, became the first American soldier since the Civil War to die before a firing squad for desertion, the lone American in World War II to die in such a context. It was not a proud moment for anyone.

Calvin Trillin,
Henry Mencken,
and Julian Bond

April 23, 1979

Calvin Marshall Trillin is a trick. Let me admit that he is an old college classmate. I assert in my defense no control over what a college admissions office may commit.

Trillin is a committer of hoaxes (pronounced HO-axes). It was just about this time last year, in fact, when Bud Trillin, as he is often known to those who admit knowing him, wrote a column in the *Nation*, one of the several outlaw publications in which his writing appears, and asserted that he had discovered a remarkably prophetic quotation from H. L. Mencken that had been "making the rounds of Washington egg-head circles lately." The alleged quote described Henry Grady's New South, according to Trillin, pegging it as "depressingly similar to the Old Middle-West." Now, Mencken was as bright a satirical writer as there was around in the 1920s and 1930s, and few things gave him more joy than sticking it to the South, Old or New. Trillin is of that same school. He spent a year as a *Time* reporter in the South in the early 1960s and went away frustrated because he once did an interview with Griffin Bell and decided afterward that he (Trillin) had not understood a single complete sentence.

Well, in the *Nation* column, Trillin went on to say that he had discovered a Mencken quote apparently coined decades ago with President Jimmy Carter's administration in mind. It read in part, "On those dark moments when I fear that the Republic has trotted before these weary eyes every carnival act in its repertoire, I cheer myself with the thought that someday we will have a President from the deserts of the Deep South. The President's Cousin, LaVerne, will travel the Hallelujah circuit as one of Mrs. McPherson's soldiers in Christ, praying for the conversion of some Northern Sodom's most Satanic pornographer as she waves his work—well thumbed—for all the yokels to gasp at. . . . The incumbent himself, cleansed of his bumpkin ways by some of Grady's New South hucksters, will have a charm comparable to that of the leading undertaker of Dothan, Alabama." There were a couple of other references in the full quote too, references that could be read as referring to First Brother Billy and even daughter Amy.

I distrusted the quote because it seemed too pat, not to mention my own direct personal knowledge of Trillin's character. James Kilpatrick later wrote a column about the Trillin Ho-ax, in admiring fashion, but noted that he kept the quote on his desk for a couple of days, "sniffing it warily now and then, and by the third day the fishy smell could not be mistaken." Mencken could indeed have written such things about a Southern president, opined Kilpatrick, but the reference to Northern Sodom's "satanic pornographer" struck the wrong note. There were not any Larry Flynt publications around in the 1920s, but Mencken crusaded in favor of those writers most criticized for language and daring.

Senator Julian Bond, who views the Carter folk with the same enthusiasm as Trillin, reprinted the quote in a column for the *Atlanta Gazette*. A *Los Angeles Times* reporter decided to take the whole thing seriously and try to find out if the quote were really from Mencken, at which point Bond jumped ship and blamed it all on Trillin. Trillin responded by asserting that he was shocked and amazed by Bond's suggestion, though noting that "there was a possibility that the person who passed the quotation on to me, a person I have refused to say was or was not Zbigniew Brzezinski, had taken advantage of my trusting nature." Bond wrote that it was clear Trillin was driven to make up quotations because of an earlier embarrassment about being taken in by the Seal Boy Hoax in 1960. Trillin wrote, "Only last month, in the course of interviewing a visiting specialist on the subject (me), the *Kansas City Star* finally printed the truth about the Seal Boy Hoax. 'The Seal Boy Hoax (a boy who supposedly lived with dolphins in the Gulf of Mexico) was a confusion Bond took for real,' the *Star* article said. 'He reported it, and then blamed Trillin when the truth was made known.' "

Senator Bond contended in reply that of course he pretended to believe in Seal Boy; it was a "cleverly concealed plan to transmit messages to underground cells of white moderates working in the civil rights movement in the early 60s, and only Mr. (J. Edgar) Hoover's death now permits the story to be told. (How that man has been maligned!)" Bond, who knows how to go for the jugular, also knows that Trillin derives some of his dubious livelihood from writing articles and books about food, roughly sixty percent of which involve the supposedly excellent barbecue in Kansas City. If the truth be told, Bond declared, he had an affidavit in hand swearing that Trillin "eats only at restaurants where the waiters can't speak English. And simper!" Where will it all end?

IRS Audits
Are Just
Coincidental

September 16, 1979[*]

Mr. John W. Henderson
District Director
Internal Revenue Service
275 Peachtree St. N.E.
Atlanta, Ga. 30303

Dear Director Henderson:

Do you have to be an IRSOB to work for the IRS? Now, I want you to know that I personally do not believe that, Mr. Henderson. I feel indeed that you have helped make it possible for me to meet a number of IRS employees over the past couple of years, and I want to assure you that they have on the whole been both courteous and helpful. I have spent a little more time than I might have chosen running down various records to prepare for my assorted sessions and correspondence, but I

---

*This essay originally appeared in the Sunday *Atlanta Journal and Constitution*.

will say it has been an interesting experience. You remember, don't you, our first conversation about IRSOBs?

There was a congressional hearing going on in Washington at the time and some folk were asserting that IRS people were being told to collect a certain "quota" in back taxes. That is, if an IRS employee spent *x* amount of time reviewing tax returns, the employee was expected to produce *x* amount of new tax money for good ol' Uncle Sam.

The IRS officially denied that such nonsense could be taking place, and I want you to know, Mr. Henderson, that I really do want to believe the official version. It was unfortunate, of course, that that IRS memo turned up saying almost exactly that: certain quotas were expected.

Anyway, you remember the editorial in the *Atlanta Constitution*, the one raising that question, do you have to be an IRSOB to work for the IRS? We ended up having quite a conversation about it, you and I, and our Executive Editor Bill Fields.

Under the circumstances, with that IRS memo kicking around and all that, we did not really feel that we should take it back and I remember that you were a little upset. Looking back, I can see now that I was certainly foolish not to do whatever you suggested. You had with you that day a scrapbook of news stories from the paper, many of them Associated Press wire stories not written by our own staffers, and I recall your feeling that the newspaper was trying to portray the IRS in a bad light.

I listened to you politely, please remember. As I have always said, just because you are paranoid, that does not mean somebody isn't still out to get you.

I didn't actually hear from you in the next few days or weeks. It was some months later, about income-tax-paying time in 1975, when I got the letter saying that the IRS wanted to audit my 1973 and 1974 tax returns. I had never been audited before, nor had my financial situation changed in any special fashion; so I must tell you that some of my more cynical colleagues felt that this sequence of events might not have been coincidence. I discount that. If your folk say so, I really want to believe that the big IRS computer in the sky turned up my name for an audit accidentally.

My colleague Bill Shipp is terribly cynical about these things. He remembers that column he wrote a little earlier this year, explaining how you once sent a special IRS agent down to help talk Betty Talmadge into paying some capital-gains tax on a land deal. You remember? That was the land that Sen. Herman Talmadge once swore was a gift to his wife and then later swore that it was only being held in trust. I want you to understand my feelings now. If a senior senator can't get special help from the IRS, why, who can?

Shipp, however, does tend to be cynical. Shortly after that column, he got word from the IRS that he was to be audited. No doubt his name too was just turned up at random by the big computer.

Well, anyway, it took some time, but I have closed out the IRS audits of my 1973 and 1974 tax returns and just the week before last I finished up with your friendly folk on 1976. I got the letter this last week that one of your examiners wants to look at my 1977 and 1978 tax returns too, but I am getting used to it all by now.

What I really wanted to say, Mr. Henderson, is that I believe your at-random explanation of all this. I just want you to know that I am on your side.

Respectfully,
Hal

We Didn't
Wait
for the Sheep

October 24, 1979

CAIRO, EGYPT—A visiting fireman has a certain responsibility to try the local wine or favorite food, almost a cultural
obligation you might say. Some might say that. There will be a
lot of belly dancing, was what Nick Tatro, the local Associated
Press guru actually said, as he and his wife offered to take a
couple of visiting journalists out to Sahara City for the
evening.

Sahara City? Well, it didn't sound much like Rock City, and
after all you can argue that in Egypt belly dancing can be considered the local delicacy. Almost a cultural requirement to go
take a look.

Not just belly dancing, the AP man's wife assured, as we
started out for the desert (yes, the desert). There's a lot of that,
but a lot of other things too. The show goes on forever, all night
long, she said. They'd stayed once until 5 in the morning and
the acts were still being introduced.

There would be tourists but also a lot of Egyptians. Once,
they had been there on a holiday night when it seemed only
Egyptians were there, most with families and children, who

got carried away with the occasion and began pelting each other with paper wads. Yes, paper wads.

But there is belly dancing? asked a colleague.

Yes, yes, was the answer, but a lot of other things too.

Wait until you see the sheep act.

The sheep act? I did not ask, I was pretty sure I did not even want to know.

The drive out to the desert was worth it, past the pyramids and the sphinx with lights outlining those ancient wonders against the sky. Sahara City turned out to be a big tent with several small buildings adjoining, the buildings turning out to be the kitchen and restrooms and such minor necessities.

There was a fair-sized stage inside the tent with tables starting right next to the stage and moving farther away. Dinner was a standard fee, about $10 per head, but the location of your table depended on the negotiated price of the bottle of whiskey (a good Scotch) that came with the table. Our group went for the $75 bottle and got a table at ringside.

There were belly dancers all right, of reasonably plump belly dimensions; it is not considered an asset here to be too thin. There were also young men dancing furiously and trying to hit each other with sticks; and singers singing furiously as if they were being beaten by sticks; two men who came out dressed as a horse and did a little number with one belly dancer; a foursome billed as "African dancers" who wore skirts like thatched huts; two aging magicians who did things with pigeons and blindfolds; and a limbo dancer who swished under the stick lower than I have ever seen it done, the stick in flames yet.

The cultural high point for me was when two of the preliminary belly dancers (as opposed to the prettier ones later) came out together and shimmied and shammied to a fare-thee-well. Then, two wooden tables were plunked down, one in front of each belly dancer, and they shimmied some more. It was somehow clear that the tables were going to be part of the act. And I began to worry about the sheep again. The tables were wooden, about four feet wide, a table leg at each corner.

Suddenly, the two dancers bent as one and each clasped her table between her teeth at the middle of one side, lifted it overhead, and began dancing wildly while holding and balancing the table overhead at the same time. There was a sign, "Sahara City," painted on the bottom of each table.

The crowd went wild. Wait until you see the act with the transvestite dwarf, murmured one of our hosts. Well, as luck would have it, we only lasted until about 2 A.M. and never got to see the dwarf act, though I am sure it was done in good taste. A shame, but we missed the sheep too. All in the shadows of the pyramids.

U. S. Governors
in Irish Dash

May 12, 1976

DUBLIN—It is not likely that there has been any other Bicentennial event quite like it, in America or Ireland; and it is most unlikely that the wide, luxurious green lawn behind the American ambassador's residence will ever be the site for quite such a scene again. It was a show, friends.

There were three governors of American states, plus the lieutenant governor of South Carolina for good measure, lining up for a footrace across that spacious lawn, even though they were dressed up in most unfootrace-like clothes, the sort of clothes you might wear to a reception in your honor being given by the American ambassador to Ireland.

Georgia Gov. George Busbee didn't plan to enter the race. He is a camera nut, is Busbee, and he was standing just a few feet away snapping pictures, coattail flying in the breeze as he shifted about trying to get a photo of the about-to-race governors that would show their faces as they crouched in sprinter's position ready for the signal to charge.

The Honorable Governor of New Jersey, Brendan T. Byrne, started the trouble when he challenged New Hampshire Gov. Meldrim Thomson, Jr.

Thomson is over sixty now, but he used to be a runner and he wasn't going to let that kind of challenge go by, certainly not from a Democrat; so they made a quick dash and both insisted the results were inconclusive. This time they decided to do it right and so a young Irish diplomat was dispatched down the field (broad green lawn, that is) to hold up a handkerchief and drop it when the winner crossed the line.

Governors Byrne and Thomson shed their coats for the great event (Byrne in bright red plaid slacks, thank you) and got down in supersprinter position. The gorgeous appeal of it all became too much for Massachusetts Gov. Michael S. Dukakis, who is a morning jogger anyway, and the Bay State one jumped in and challenged the first two and got himself hunkered down into position.

At that point Connecticut Gov. Ella T. Grasso (call her Governor; she'll get mad if you call her Mrs., another governor confided) decided to start the race in proper fashion with a "ready, get set, on your mark, go." The trouble with all that is that it amounts to four separate commands, and New Hampshire Gov. Thomson couldn't wait that long, not for four different commands, his arms swinging back and forth as he crouched ready to dash. He would start running somewhere between "get set" and "on your mark" and the other governors would make him come back and play fair. Then Pennsylvania Gov. Milton J. Shapp came over to exert his authority as the sort-of-spokesman for the group and said, "Come on, Ella, let's get 'em started." He was prepared to take charge of getting it started, but Gov.-Mrs. Grasso was having none of that and she effectively pressed the governor of Pennsylvania aside and prepared to do "ready, get set" and all the rest yet again.

The lieutenant governor of South Carolina, W. Brantley Harvey, found himself tempted by the devil and the delay, so he quickly shed his coat and charged over to line up with the other about-to-be-sprinters. This time Gov. Thomson managed to restrain himself until the word "go" and the Four Horsemen of the Governors' Party began their sprint, heads down and legs churning.

Massachusetts Gov. Dukakis looked pretty good coming off the mark, head down and getting some power into his stride, but on about the first good solid stepping out, his leather shoe slipped on that abundant, thick green grass and he went head over heels, landing on his shoulder and breaking his collarbone (or separating his shoulder, equally painful).

The three still in the running pressed on. Gov. Thomson fell a little behind the other two, having spotted them both a decade plus in years, and Gov. Byrne and Lt. Gov. Harvey ended up in what appeared a dead heat. The governor of New Jersey claimed victory nonetheless, and the lieutenant governor of South Carolina smiled good-humoredly and deferred to rank.

The unlikely sprint was a high point of a three-day visit by ten American governors, plus representatives of the governors of three other states, all the 200-years-later political survivors of the original thirteen American colonies. It was all planned, yes, believe it or not, as Ireland's way of celebrating this nation's bicentennial. The only comparable moment, in a way, was maybe that evening at the Abbey Tavern at the Hill of Howth when Gov. Shapp and Lt. Gov. Harvey doffed their coats, not for a race this time, but to borrow the fiddles of the musical group at the tavern and play their version of "When Irish Eyes Are Smiling."

The governors' visit to Ireland had its serious sides, some worth writing about later, such as the pleas of Irish government officials for our cooperation in blocking American moneys contributed to factions in Northern Ireland, moneys that end up buying guns and bombs.

There were also serious overtones involving Irish hopes for greater American investment and greater numbers of American tourists to the Emerald Isle. But on the whole it was as good-humored and lighthearted a bicentennial visit as can be imagined. Irish-American ties survived it all in good order.

Strolling Around
the Yale Campus

April 29, 1980[15]

NEW HAVEN—"It is like being the mayor of a town," said Bart Giamatti while strolling around Yale University campus one sunny afternoon last week, greeting people and being greeted as often as any High Mayor might during a walk through the streets of his city.

Yale University is Giamatti's city and community. He became the nineteenth president of Yale in 1978 when he was forty years old, the youngest president of the university in more than 200 years.

Giamatti's mustache and closely cropped beard give him a slightly Machiavellian look, a bit dashing. Give him the right costume and he could easily pass for a nobleman in Dante's

---

[15]When I was young and clearheaded (say, about age thirteen), I kept up with major league baseball pretty well. More recently, my limited expertise has involved only keeping up with the Atlanta Braves. Bart Giamatti keeps up better than I do. I wrote, in error, that Bart's article, "Tom Seaver's Farewell," was written on the occasion of Seaver's retirement from baseball. Actually, it was written when Seaver was traded to another team and forced reluctantly to leave New York.

Florence. He might like that, in fact. His field of scholarship has been Medieval and Renaissance literature, and Dante and Provencal poetry are among his special interests.

Just outside Woolsey Hall, not far from his office, are a small band of protestors with guitars and signs. They are against nuclear power and against the draft. Nobody seems to be paying them much attention. It is not like the wrenching and often bitter student demonstrations of the 1960s and Giamatti, for one, is glad that college campuses around the country are currently back to a kind of routine, back to the chance to nourish excellence in teaching and scholarship without continuing campus controversy.

Not that Giamatti dodges controversy or hesitates to speak out. Presidential candidate Ronald Reagan got caught out a bit in telling a mild ethnic joke in New Hampshire, one about a duck at a cock fight that had some negative mention of Poles and Italians. Giamatti is proud of his Italian-American heritage (his father, Valentine Giamatti, is professor emeritus of Italian at Mount Holyoke College) and issued a terse statement from the Yale president's office. Reagan, he said, should apologize even to the ducks.

You can even make a case that, for a soft-spoken, benign-appearing fellow, Giamatti creates his share of controversy. He made a speech at his official inauguration suggesting that there was, after all, "hierarchy" in a major university, a necessary structure for administration and decision making, and that finally the president of the university had to make a good many of the final decisions. Some faculty members and students reacted as if Giamatti had seriously suggested a new Spanish Inquisition.

More recently, he made a speech suggesting that it might be well to take a hard look at athletics at Yale and other Ivy League colleges, that there was a need maybe for some further guidelines for postseason games and in other areas. Outraged alumni who thought they heard that dreaded word to college sports fans, "deemphasize" (though in fact the word was not in the speech), have been protesting ever since.

Actually, Giamatti is a sports buff in his own right, especially a big baseball fan. He wrote an article when Tom Seaver retired from professional baseball, "Tom Seaver's Farewell," which ran in *Harper's* and then in an anthology of best sports stories of 1978.

Walking around the Yale campus with the university's nineteenth president is interesting. He runs into the provost and they remind each other of an 8 P.M. meeting that night at someone's house. A student shouts something about his favorite baseball team and Giamatti predicts bad things for the Orioles this season. A student taking a tour group around the campus stops so that the group can take a look at the president of Yale.

Around one corner he runs into a young faculty member and there is a small, serious chat. Giamatti has talked to the man at length earlier, trying to get him to accept an important post in the university hierarchy; but the faculty member is frankly not certain that he wants to give up what he is now doing to take on the other job. It is not resolved on the spot. The faculty member promises to talk to another colleague about the matter, then to talk again to Giamatti.

The president of a major university these days must concern himself with an array of difficult problems, everything from security on the campus to student discipline to how soaring energy costs and inflation can tear apart the most carefully planned budgets. Giamatti shakes his head over one of the newer buildings on the Yale campus, a tall, good-sized building, only a few years old now, but constructed before energy costs were much of a factor in designing such a building. Now, the escalating energy cost of that one building is almost enough to disrupt a budget.

If he has one prime worry, Giamatti probably thinks most often about the need to encourage excellence in teaching, which means as a start encouraging and placing high value on those individuals who choose teaching as a career. "A liberal education is at the heart of a civil society," he said in one speech, "and at the heart of a liberal education is the act of teaching."

The goal in the end, though, is that each individual, faculty member or student, becomes both teacher and student. "The human race survives despite itself in many ways," said Giamatti, "but it survives because of itself when it passes on the best of its past and the best of its aspiration through the open sharing of the blood and sinew of the mind. That moment of poise, when what is known becomes accessible and must then become what is to be found, is the act of teaching, and those acts in sequence are a life, in which, once we learn how, we are all teachers and students of ourselves."

All Hail
Conquering
Columbia

April 15, 1981

Mankind's exploration of space moved into a new era this week with the successful mission of the American space shuttle Columbia.

Americans can feel pride indeed about the success of the mission. It was the first American-manned space flight in more than five years; the first flight in known human history of a spacecraft that could soar from the Earth and then land again and may be flown again after that first mission.

But it was a moving into that new era for all mankind also. There will come a time in human history, assuming we don't manage to blow ourselves up first, when the latter half of the twentieth century may be viewed as primarily the time of mankind's first beginning explorations of the rest of the universe, the first tentative steps to explore greater worlds around us, both within our own solar system and to solar systems and galaxies beyond.

The beginnings may seem small centuries from now, when spacecraft voyages to planets yet undiscovered will be routine, but the future historians may well try to recapture the tensions and excitement of these first important steps.

The Soviet orbiting of an unmanned satellite in the 1950s, Sputnik, electrified the world. It may seem small potatoes now, but it was a huge technological breakthrough. It startled Americans, who had been so long convinced that no other nation could match our technology, let alone the bad old Communists. It led to the beginnings of the American space program, an instant commitment to match the Soviet technology and to put a new emphasis in this country on math and science in the public schools.

It led to the late President John F. Kennedy's pledge after the 1960 presidential election that the United States would seek to land a man on the moon by the end of the decade. That was a pledge fulfilled.

There were some funny things in that time. German rocket scientists from World War II were the best in the world, the most knowledgeable about those things that tied into the embryonic space technology. Wernher von Braun headed the American space effort; other German scientists were working for the Russians.

Americans worked feverishly to catch up to the Soviets, and some thought with good humor, "our Germans against their Germans." The Germans took some amusement in all that, too. One West German newspaper ran a cartoon in that period of a Russian and an American satellite orbiting the Earth, one around the other. The caption, in German, of course, read: "When do we start speaking our native tongue?"

The triumph of the space shuttle Columbia is a wondrous one. All hail to the two brave men who broke new ground in the skies, and to the many, many technicians and scientists and workers who took part in that triumph.

It is part of a new era. The space shuttle will be able to carry astronauts and scientists to existing satellites for repairs, or even to bring them back to Earth, or to place new satellites with precision in space. There is the mundane side to it: in a happy fashion, the notion that this part of exploration in space is on the way to becoming ordinary—ordinary, at least, in the sense of becoming as safe as an ordinary plane ride, making possible great steps forward in the further development of space technology.

Americans have reason for pride in the space shuttle Columbia. So do the rest of the people living on this globe.

A Saga
of *Playboy*
and Baylor

*June 7, 1981**

This is a saga of *Playboy* magazine and Baylor University and how that, no doubt (in the eyes of Baylor officials) ungodly, publication placed temptation in the paths of Baylor coeds, urging them to bare their bodies.

It is also a tale, beyond the threat of corruption of pure Baptist girls in Waco, Texas, of the First Amendment and college newspapers and a couple of young journalists who actually thought that even on a Baptist campus the college newspaper ought to be able to criticize the administration of the college. Ah, foolish thought.

That may all sound a bit exaggerated. It should. The story is real enough though, even if exaggerated. And it has another dimension, one that involves Ralph McGill, late distinguished publisher and editor of the *Atlanta Constitution*. He is known fondly as "Revolving Ralph" to some of us who read letters to

*This essay originally appeared in the Sunday *Atlanta Journal and Constitution*.

the *Atlanta Constitution*; an incredible number of letter writers out there are convinced that the late editor McGill would, as the phrase goes, turn over in his grave to know what we are saying on a certain issue. The folks who knew McGill best tend not to be quite so presumptuous; you can value a man's ideals and courage in his time, but how can you assert with authority what he might say on a complex issue that comes along more than a decade after his death?

Anyway, *Playboy* magazine decided to visit Waco and the Baylor University environs to interview comely coeds who might want to consider posing for photographs in that magazine. The president of Baylor, one Abner V. McCall, declared that any Baylor gal who appeared nude or seminude in *Playboy* would face serious disciplinary action. The campus newspaper, the *Lariat*, editorialized that the individual young woman (ah, heavens, what boldness) should decide on such matters even if she happened to be a student at Baylor. "To pose or not to pose, that is the question—a clear and simple issue now buried somewhere under a mudslide of moralism precipitated by a new rain of fundamentalist politics," said the campus newspaper, adding for good measure that if the tempted coed "is mature enough to understand her own needs, her own inhibitions, her own qualms, and her own mischievousness, then show us the harm in her posing."

Ah, sin had struck at the heart of Baylor. Or so the university authorities believed. President McCall viewed the whole thing as a threat of "pornography" and the campus newspaper as being on the side of the devil.

The editor, Jeff Barton, and the news editor, Cyndy Slovak, and others on the newspaper staff found all this a bit hard to believe. They appealed to McCall, to their faculty advisers, to the student publications board. The sequence was fairly incredible and too complex to relate in detail. The upshot was that the Baylor officials fired the editors of the *Lariat*, complaining that they were, in the words of McCall's statement, "denying the basic tenets of the Christian faith. . . ."

The reporting and editorials in that campus newspaper were, on review, pretty straightforward. There were no exploitative uses of profanity or salaciousness or anything with the *Playboy* magazine theme as a base. Pretty mild stuff, except for one thing: the students putting out their campus newspaper dared to challenge the smug assumptions of the Baylor administration; they actually tried to put out a responsible newspaper.

The editors were fired from the publication. Students supported them overwhelmingly, despite that. Two Baylor journalism professors resigned in general embarrassment over the empty-headed actions of the administration. Students on the newspaper with Baylor scholarships had those scholarships taken away.

This gets back to Ralph McGill. Today is the announcement date for awarding next year's McGill scholarships in journalism. The awards committee awarded two of those scholarships to Jeff Barton, former editor of the *Lariat*, and to Cyndy Slovak, former news editor. The two earned the awards on the basis of record and ability. But the members of the awards committee were not unmindful of the Baylor-*Playboy* controversy and felt, indeed, that those two young journalists and their fellow staffers had handled themselves with intelligence, dignity, and a high degree of professional journalistic competence in a most difficult situation.

It is presumptuous, of course, in a way. But the members of the Ralph McGill scholarship awards committee felt that ole Revolving Ralph would have rather enjoyed the notion of these two bright young journalists receiving such awards in his name. They have left Baylor, by the way. The two plan to be married this summer. They are both now attending the University of Texas in Austin.

Good Words
Engage
a "Friendly Tongue"

January 8, 1982

There was a great occasion at lunch Wednesday in the Biltmore Hotel in Atlanta, appreciated by those there who love books and the use of words.

The event probably would have pleased the fellow in whose name the luncheon was given. Jim Townsend was a crafty, articulate, silver-tongued devil, quite capable of convincing any writer that he or she was just on the verge of producing something absolutely splendid. He often made it happen, too, seemingly being able to talk and con almost anyone out of any alleged form of writer's block. Townsend founded *Atlanta* magazine twenty years ago and made it the best magazine of its kind in the country. He was something of an inspiration for writers at every publication he touched, full of ideas and notions and provocative talk.

Townsend died of cancer last year. The luncheon Wednesday was to celebrate the first Townsend Fiction Prize, given to an Atlanta author whose book was published this past year. Celestine Sibley of this newspaper won the first award, against some strong competition, and there was a nice touch in that for those of us who admire her abundant talent; no one in Atlanta has worked any harder to use words well, to craft phrases and paragraphs, whether in a straightforward, tough-minded news story on a murder case, or in her columns or fiction.

The author delivering the luncheon speech was in exceptionally good form, though the literary role is just foreign enough to him to make him just a little uncomfortable.

The author was Lt. Gov. Zell Miller, whose book *The Mountains Within Me* is a fine volume, partly autobiographical, mostly about the history and customs and language and folkways of his native north Georgia. Miller grew up listening to mountain men tell tall tales and gossip about everything and use words in interesting fashion, sometimes using phrases (as Miller the college history professor would learn later) that went back centuries, to English language usage now almost forgotten.

The lieutenant governor passed on some of the phrases and stories that he still liked from that growing-up time. He once heard someone describe one man as "such a liar" that the man had to get somebody else to call up his hogs.

There was talk one day of a woman in town who had, shall we say, a somewhat doubtful reputation. One man finally spoke up for her, at least more or less, suggesting that he did not want to make a judgment about the woman. "I'm no judge and there's not enough of me to be a jury," he allowed.

Miller talked too about a "mountain writer" who had been his friend, the poet Byron Herbert Reece. He farmed and wrote his poetry and taught at Young Harris and won considerable recognition. He became ill and depressed, and one June night in 1958, at the age of forty, he put a favorite record on the phonograph and then shot himself.

There is a brass plaque in a cover on Blood Mountain, said Miller, with a quote from one of Reece's verses:

From chips and shards in idle times
I made these stories, shaped these rhymes
May they engage some friendly tongue
When I am past the reach of song.

That is also what Jim Townsend's love of words was all about, concluded Miller, the fact that the carefully crafted words live on after the writer has passed from the earthly scene, live on to be enjoyed by "some friendly tongue."

Twenty Years
of Memories
Will Remain

June 18, 1982

This is my last column for the *Atlanta Constitution*, and I find I write it in good cheer, though with regret at leaving a great newspaper.

An editor has a rare opportunity to view significant events of the time at close range, and sometimes even to influence those events. That's the greatest and glorious part. There is the less glamorous part, too, such as the daily routine and the kooks and cranks. But it gets down to something like this: if you don't absolutely enjoy most of the job most of the time, you are crazy to be working in this business at all. My luck has been to enjoy it thoroughly and to have a ringside seat at some of the more remarkable happenings of the past two decades.

It was just about twenty years ago, in the summer of 1962, that I came to the *Atlanta Constitution* as a reporter. No one could have really imagined the trauma and drama of the years to follow. John Kennedy was in the White House, with only a little over a year left before the murderous attack in Dallas would claim his life. Martin Luther King, Jr. was in Atlanta, already the national leader of the civil rights revolution. Neither King nor Robert Kennedy, then attorney general, would live out the decade. Vietnam? Watergate? Neither word meant much then, though both would come to have searing impact on our national life.

That year of 1962 was an interesting political year for Georgia. Two young lawyers scored stunning upset election victories: Carl Sanders as governor, and Charlie Weltner as Fifth District congressman from Atlanta. Both were energetic, progressive, impressive. It seemed a good omen for another New South, one looking more to the future than the past. It is a measure of how recently that was that both Sanders and Weltner are still very much active and around—Sanders as a highly successful attorney and power in the Democratic party, and Weltner as a justice on the Georgia Supreme Court.

There was someone else who started a political career that year of 1962, a fellow named Jimmy Carter, from Plains, Georgia, who got elected to the State Senate. Whatever became of him, anyway?

I was properly cynical as a young reporter. I knew there were thieves and knaves about, skulduggery, bad people in the world. There are, too. But I must report that I find myself after these twenty years far more optimistic about the human condition than when I started out. There are an extraordinary number of people around with good motivations, people who work hard at what they do and who go out of their way to be helpful to others, often without any special appreciation.

I have found that to be true also in the areas where I have been much involved, in politics and government and in the media. Newspapers are often taken to task for running too many negative stories—and there is some truth in that—but a great part of the reason is that these bad-news stories are of interest because they are out of the ordinary. A story about a crooked politician is almost routine. One of the delights in my job has been to discover how many public men and women are honest and hard-working, subject to more temptations than most of us, and yet on the whole committed to excellence and to fulfilling their responsibilities in honest fashion.

I have found the same thing with newspaper people, both in Atlanta and around the country. A daily newspaper by definition is a guarantee of some mistakes and errors, simply because the newspaper comes out every day of the week. We make mistakes on occasion and usually try hard to correct them. But, Lord knows, the journalists I've known with newspapers are in the business because they value the craft and try hard to work at it conscientiously. There is no contempt more deepset than that a good reporter holds for some other journalist who clearly has done a slipshod job on a story.

No editor ever had a stouter supporter or friend than Jack Tarver, who was publisher when I took on the job. He could steady your soapbox with authority, a fellow with as good newspaper instincts as anyone I know.

My experience indeed has been rich in talented colleagues. There is a temptation to list so many, and the trouble is that there is almost no end to it. But some have meant a great deal in my life. I count Tarver and Bill Shipp, Jim Minter and Bill Fields (the only fellow I know who ever made the mistake of hiring me twice). Reg Murphy, editor while I was associate editor, has been a colleague and friend since we both worked for the *Macon Telegraph*; we even managed to remain friends while Jimmy Carter was in the White House, no small feat.

Lists make dull reading, but my experience as editor has been a glorious one, in part because of the chance to get to know some of my brethren in the trade throughout the country.

Jack Nelson delights because he is evidence that a Mississippi lad can work for the *Atlanta Constitution* and then go to Washington to become as good a reporter as there is in that town, which is aswim with journalists. Abe Rosenthal of the *New York Times* inspires because he puts out what is probably, on any given day, the best newspaper in the world. Bob White of the *Mexico Ledger* in Missouri shows you that you can run a small newspaper and be just as involved in national and international issues as anyone. Well, there are too many to name. Johnny Popham from Chattanooga, Tom Winship from Boston, Claude Sitton in Raleigh, David Laventhol with *News-*

day, John Seigenthaler in Nashville . . . these have been friends and colleagues; I have learned from them.

I have learned from you too, gentle reader. That has been one of the continuing joys of the job, the constant dialogue between readers and an editor. There may be someone out there who has hesitated to write to me or call on the telephone. There can't be too many.

The very first column I wrote as editor ran on September 1, 1975, and I wrote of my pride at being associated with a newspaper of character and tradition with a history of standing for something. I wrote too that there was something people should understand about a newspaper, namely, that the owners and managers could obviously have whatever kind of editors and news executives they wanted, strong and independent-minded—even daring—or the milksop variety. I can report accurately that no editor has had more freedom and support than I've had these last years, or more encouragement to take on the controversial issues.

It's been fun.

Index